THE GANGSTERS

THE GANGSTERS

Timothy Jacobs

MALLARD
PRESS

First published in the United States of America in 1990 by
The Mallard Press
Mallard Press and its accompanying design and logo are
trademarks of BDD Promotional Book Company, Inc.

ISBN 0-792-45269-0

Printed in Hong Kong

Designed by Ruth DeJauregui
Captioned by Timothy Jacobs

Page 1: Bonnie Parker was one half of the ruthless duo known as Bonnie and Clyde, the leaders of 'the Barker Gang.' Bonnie and her partner, Clyde Barrow, often sent photographs of themselves to the newspapers for fun. This photo shows Bonnie with a cigar in her mouth—something she thought would enhance the 'joke' quality of the image, but which fixed her in the popular imagination as a cigar-smoking gun moll.

Page 2: The Charlie Birger Gang.

These pages: Manhattan in the 1930s. New York City was the home base for Salvatore Lucania, alias Charlie 'Lucky' Luciano, who instituted organized crime as we now know it.

TABLE OF CONTENTS

Al Capone and His Underworld   6

Lucky Luciano and His Underworld   54

Infamous Rural and Suburban Outlaws   80

John Dillinger   80

Pretty Boy Floyd   84

Baby Face Nelson   85

Ma Barker and Her Boys   86

Machine Gun Kelly   88

Bonnie and Clyde   89

Index   94

Al Capone and His Underworld

Alphonse Capone was born in New York City on 17 January 1899. He was the son of Gabriel and Teresa Capone, who had emigrated from the slums of Naples, Italy to New York City a few years before. For much of young Alphonse's boyhood, the family lived in an apartment on Navy Street in Brooklyn, in the midst of the biggest Italian ghetto in New York at the time. Many immigrants had been peasants in their former country, and their largely agrarian skills meant little in the middle of teeming New York City. Capone's father, a barber, was only slightly better off.

While many immigrants were imbued with a deep and positive morality, a number of them were in service to the underworld—with its allure of quick profit, unearned respect and amoral power. Like a plague it followed them wherever they went—even into the 'New World' of America—seen as a promised land of sorts where they hoped to leave such terrors behind, and to build their lives anew, without such oppression.

But the underworld saw America as yet more territory, and did battle with the Irish, Polish and Jewish gangs that already existed in the US. In Italy, the underworld was organized into several organizations: the Neapolitan Camorra, the Sicilian Mafia and the Calabrian Carbonari. In America, Italian gangs were established along the same lines. Gradually, these conformations were severely tested and altered, as increasing numbers of 'independent' operators (who would eventually include Capone) began to establish gangs with a broader ethnic membership.

No matter its formal evolution, this very underworld kept many of the Italian immigrants poor. The mob collector paid a visit to each apartment in a New York ghetto tenement—and exacted a fee for the privilege of the household's right to live another day. This was called 'protection money.'

Many immigrant parents taught their children that the only way out of the trap was by way of the free public education system that America offered, whereby any youngster, despite prejudice, could hope to better himself sufficiently to be out of the grasp of the Mafia thugs.

Still, some of the immigrant kids, as some kids anywhere, resented school. Unfortunately, their diversion was no swimmin' hole or country fair, but the dismal street life of the ghetto.

Young Alphonse Capone heard the siren song and followed it. He was big for his age, and full of braggadocio and swagger. Even so, it was observed that the boy Capone only needed a little more willpower to develop his fascination with the US Navy ships that docked regularly at the end of Navy Street. He had the ability to lead, and might have had a legitimate career as an officer. It was not to be: there was a weakness in him that he refused to combat. Though his was to become the most notorious name in the annals of American crime, he would never truly rise above the gutter mentality of the Mafia-infected ghetto streets.

The Capones left Navy Street in 1907, moving about a mile south, to 38 Garfield Place. The deceptively mild-looking Johnny Torrio, among other thugs, was very prominent in this new neighborhood. His center of operations, disguised as a social club called 'The John Torrio Association' was an induction center for neighborhood gangs, where weak-willed, passionately unruly youngsters were drawn into the life of the underworld.

Below: **European immigrants, thronging the deck of a ship as it pulls into New York Harbor.** *At right:* **Alphonse 'Al' Capone.**

Alphonse attended PS 133 and maintained a B average up to the sixth grade, but fell behind due to his own increasing truancy. He flunked sixth grade and, during his second year at that level, punched a young female teacher. The principal of the school administered a spanking, and Alphonse Capone—setting a course that he would follow for the rest of his life—left school for good, feeling that he was somehow above being accountable for his own actions.

For a while, he worked as a clerk in a candy store, next became a pin setter in a bowling alley, and then as a paper and cloth cutter in a bindery. On the side, he was a small time bully, threatening school children for their lunch money. Then he met Torrio, and was introduced into the Five Pointers, a notoriously violent gang that was based in Manhattan's Lower East Side.

The Five Pointers specialized in murder and mayhem, and offered their services for a fee, as is witnessed by the following 'menu':

Punching	$ 2
Both eyes blacked	4
Nose and jaw broke	10
Jacked out (knocked out with a black jack)	15
Ear chawed off	15
Leg or arm broke	19
Shot in leg	25
Stab	25
Doing the big job	100

A union racketeer and ex-bantamweight prizefighter known in the underworld as 'Paul Kelly' (true name, Paolo Antonini Vacarelli) was the leader of the Five Pointers, and from his New Brighton Dance Hall in Manhattan's Great Jones Street, he directed the operations of some 1500 Five Pointer thugs. The Five Pointers lay claim to all the territory between The Bowery and Broadway, and Fourteenth Street and City Hall.

Kelly had protection from reekingly corrupt Tammany Hall, who found his thugs useful in 'enforcing' votes at election time. However, long-term warfare with an even more violent gang, run by the bestial 'Monkeyface' Eastman,

Below: **A cartoon symbolic of corruption.** ***At right:*** **Grand Central Station, Chicago's early gateway for millions, including mobsters.**

had resulted in Kelly's self-serving departure from the street gang scene.

Kelly kept at a distance from the Five Pointers, but always stayed close enough to call them, and after the gang's old headquarters was shut down, set up a new one for them near the Broadway Theater District, with the misleading moniker of 'The New Englander Social and Dramatic Club.' The Five Pointers operated out of this headquarters, carrying on their main business of robbery, assault and murder for hire.

Whenever the police raided, there was nothing more suspicious that 'a few fellows sitting around, engaged in a game of checkers.' Young Alphonse, big for his age and possessed of a violent temper, was soon neck-deep in this gang of thugs. During his days as a Five Pointer, he was arrested three times—once for disorderly conduct and twice for homicide—but the charges were bought off. Capone was by now in full flight toward his distorted vision of the 'easily gotten riches' of the New World.

Young Capone's increasing brutality soon attracted the attention of Frank Uale, aka 'Frankie Yale,' the overlord of Brooklyn racketeering. Yale knew the old Mafia Don Cirro Terranova personally, and had emulated the older man in his far-reaching, societally parasitical activities. Yale's enterprises, among others, were rum-running from coastal fleets during Prohibition, extortion, protection, union busting, management busting, and forcing shop owners to handle goods from his suppliers, including terrible low-grade cigars, made with sawdust and other unsavory ingredients, that were priced far above their worth: these stogies were called 'Frank Yales,' and were complete with a suitably cold-eyed likeness of their namesake on the wrapper.

Race fixing and fight fixing described Yale's interest in sports, in addition to which he owned nightclubs and a funeral parlor; this latter related to one of Yale's biggest rackets—murder for hire. 'I'm an undertaker,' he often said. However, inroads that he had made upon the original Unione Siciliane provided his greatest profit and influence.

The Unione Siciliane originated as a lawful fraternal organization, designed to advance the interests of Sicilian immigrants: for a modest fee, Sicilians could get life insurance and other social benefits. There was a chapter wherever a notable population of Sicilians had gathered. The largest was in the Chicago area, with 38 lodges and 40,000 members.

The first thug to infiltrate the Unione was Ignazio Saietta, known to the underworld as 'Lupo the Wolf.' He was a psychotic killer who hung his victims on meathooks in his 'murder house' in Harlem, and then burned their bodies in a furnace. He and his minions began to infiltrate the Unione nationally, and the organization took on a schizophrenic character: one half did beneficent works, and the other, mob-controlled, specialized in robbery, murder, white slavery, extortion and murder.

Frank Yale became the President of the Unione Siciliane in the early 1920s, and his influence flowed out through its chapters across the country. Yale hired Alphonse Capone upon the recommendation of Johnny Torrio. Capone was all too useful to his new employer, having become, like him, a ruthless man, devoid of conscience. Capone was heavy and strong and a murderous fighter, and he was handy with a gun, having practiced shooting bottles in the basement of a hangout in Brooklyn.

As a return of favors, Yale loaned him back to Torrio, and he became a bouncer at Torrio's Harvard Inn, a sleazy nightclub where underworld types of all sorts hung out. One source gives this employment as the source of the scars that marked him with the nickname that he hated—'Scarface.' It seems that Capone tried to 'bounce' a fellow lowlifer who was armed with a knife, and who didn't want to be 'bounced.'

Another historian gives the source of those scars as an irate Sicilian barber who, razor in hand and temper exploding, reacted violently to Capone's attempt to 'muscle' his patrons for money. At any rate, the scars which he bore on the left side of his face were never to be photographed if Capone could help it, always requesting photographers to 'shoot' his right profile.

The man who had become his underworld 'sponsor,' Johnny Torrio, had a reputation as a criminal 'mind' (an oxymoron if there ever was one). He was soft spoken, mild mannered, short and slight. While he had personally seldom pulled a gun outright and killed anyone, he had plotted dozens of executions for a number of gangs by the time he had subsumed Capone into the Five Pointers. Torrio had no true ethical foundation, yet he abhorred unnecessary violence as a hindrance to criminal 'business,' which, he felt, generated enough profits 'for everyone.' In this, he inspired both his early protege Capone, and his later associate, Charlie 'Lucky' Luciano, who was to become the very head of the American underworld by the end of Prohibition.

Torrio saw, in young Capone, the potential to become a compunctionless, thoroughly jaded man like himself: in other words, he saw that Capone could become a true-blue gangster. It has been pointed out that, 'These people are missing a piece of their brains.' For, certainly, they think of no one but themselves—not even their own children, who have to inhabit the world that they so badly distort with their actions.

And Alphonse Capone was soon to father a child. In one of the many 'cellar' clubs where young thugs of Capone's time tended to spend their hours, Alphonse met a tall Irish girl named Mae Coughlin. While the Italian and Irish communities as a rule did not smile on one another, it was true that certain circumstances encouraged intermarriage to happen.

Italian boys had no fear of marriage, while Irish boys tended to wait until they were well settled in their occupations. Therefore, marriage-anxious Irish girls found an attraction, as did Mae Coughlin, in Italian boys. Alphonse married May almost immediately—the ceremony was performed on 18 December 1918.

A year later, Mae gave birth to their first and only child, Albert Francis Capone, affectionately known as 'Sonny.' Ironically, Johnny Torrio became the boy's godfather—traditionally a role reserved for a pious friend or relative delegated to see to the child's spiritual education.

Soon, Torrio settled permanently in Chicago, and sent for Capone. Under suspicion for two murders in New York, and with the authorities awaiting the death of a Harvard Inn patron he had savagely beaten, Capone was not hard to convince. He went to Chicago, to be with his patron in crime.

One of the chief reasons that Big Jim Colosimo had called Torrio to Chicago was protection for his racket. Colosimo was involved in the word of Chicago vice, and was especially known to be a white slaver—one who kidnapped and enslaved young women to work in brothels, a practice origi-

nated in Chicago by the sinister nineteenth century madam Mary Hastings.

Surviving an average of four years, the girls were literally worn out, and then drugs—or the street that they were thrown into like so much refuse—finished their ruined lives. This despicable 'racket' was also known as 'compulsory prostitution,' and was the very crime that would cause the downfall of the notorious Lucky Luciano in the mid-1930s.

Colosimo was also into labor racketeering, and had, by means of the votes garnered thereby, established a powerful empire, protected by ward aldermen John 'Bathhouse' Coughlin and Michael 'Hinky Dink' Kenna. In fact, they made him a precinct captain, which guaranteed his immunity from arrest, according to the corrupt political system then extant in Chicago.

Colosimo had become quite wealthy, and became a target of the 'Black Hand,' not really an organized gang, but really an established method of extorting money. That Colosimo should become a victim in his own right seems only fitting. Soon enough, the notes with the familiar black hand or skull and crossbones began to arrive by mail.

The Black Hand flourished in the Italian immigrant community, kept alive by criminals who had come over to the New World in order to further victimize their compatriots. They used bombs, knives and guns to carry out their threats, and a typical Black Hand note might read as follows:

GRAND CENTRAL STATION, HARRISON STREET AND FIFTH AVE. CHICAGO, ILL.

Most Gentle Mr Sylvani—

Hoping that the present will not impress you too much, you will be so good as to send me $2000 if your life is dear to you. So I beg you warmly to put them (sic) on the door within four days. But if not, I swear this week's time not even the dust of your family will exist. With regards, believe me to be your friend....

Reform movements time and again caused abatements in both Black Hand extortion by mail and white slavery. The problem in both cases was that the corruption simply spread itself in other directions: the Black Handers no longer wrote letters, they delivered their threat in person, or called on the phone; the white slavers simply brought in 'cargoes' of unfortunate young women from distant cities, so that tracing such 'missing persons' would be more difficult.

Colosimo, a white slaver suffering Black Hand extortion, took the matter into his own hands, laying traps for his extortioners and at least once, killing three of them. Still, he regularly found himself doling out thousands of dollars, and sent for his nephew, Johnny Torrio to help him deal with the problem full time. Throughout the decade following 1909, Torrio paid extended visits to Colosimo, finally settling in Chicago in 1920.

Torrio, the tactician, soon made Colosimo's own gang of heavies one of the most feared in Chicago. Colosimo's 'army' included brother-in-law Joe Moresco, Mac Fitzpatrick, Billy Leathers, 'Chicken Harry' Gullet and Joe 'Jew Kid' Grabiner. Black Hand threats against Colosimo were soon eliminated.

The Colosimo vice empire, plus the various saloons that Colosimo owned and his newly-formed protection racket, fell under the Torrio organizational plan. By 1920, Colosimo was the pre-eminent mobster in Chicago, protected all the way to the governor's office by the corrupt politicians that Torrio, an ardent payola master, had bought. Torrio's talents stretched into other areas as well.

Reformers such as the English evangelist Gypsy Smith brought public attention to the moral garbage heap that was Colosimo's base of operation—the Levee District. Smith, marching with an army of Chicagoans 20,000 strong, chanting the Lord's Prayer and praying for all the women entrapped in the brothels invaded the Levee in 1909. Two months later, the Federated Protestant Churches demanded that a special Morals Squad be set up.

Since that time, it had been an ongoing battle between the forces of reform and the vice rings of the Levee. A good many of the smaller operators had been shut down, in large part due to the efforts of a special Morals Squad instituted and run by Second Deputy Police Commissioner Major Metellus Funkhauser and his deputy WC Dannenberg. Still, Colosimo's graft kept him out of the reach of the law.

Even this graft protection seemed to be crumbling when the Morals Squad succeeded in lifting the liquor license from Colosimo's splendiferous nightclub, 'Colosimo's Cafe,' a glittering rhinestone of vice, set in the very center of the Levee.

Then, suddenly, it seemed that the forces of corruption had won a major victory: with the highly rigged 1915 mayoral elections, the preposterous, bellicose and entirely cor-

At right: **South Water Street in Chicago, circa 1915. Amid such scenes of hustle and bustle, the underworld could operate almost unseen—and with political corruption, could operate openly.**

rupt Big Bill Thompson—a political glutton whose cheap theatrics were directed to play strictly on unexamined emotion—was elected mayor of Chicago.

Thompson proceeded to make Chicago the most wide-open city in America. The Sportsmen's Club, a political organization, was made the collection agency for Thompson's graft: gangsters, whoremasters and gamblers, along with 'respectable' city officials, received membership request letters with the mayor's letterhead.

Thompson stripped Funkhouser and his Morals Squad of all authority. In Thompson's Chicago, when grafters were brought to trial, they were soon freed, and if not freed immediately, availed themselves of the services of Chicago's best criminal lawyers, in several cases, notably Clarence Darrow. Meanwhile, Colosimo had grown so big in the underworld that his pet aldermen now came to him for favors.

Hope dawned anew, when a federal investigation of the nationwide white slavery ring was instituted. The chief witness was a girl who was drugged in a cafe via knockout drops in her coffee. She woke up imprisoned by Colosimo's men, who abused her and then installed her in a house of prostitution. She was fortunate enough to escape—an almost impossible feat in itself.

She was sequestered by the courts in a hideout in Connecticut. There being a danger that his favorite fetid pool might be dried up, the reptilian Torrio arranged for a pair of his James Street thugs to masquerade as federal agents, who 'picked her up for transport to the courthouse,' and subsequently killed her.

Colosimo esteemed Torrio anew for this act of saving his worthless neck, and cut him in for a big share of his Chicago empire. Torrio emerged as a new power in gangland, and immediately convinced Colosimo that the Levee District was soon to see its last days. He felt the way to assure their future in abusing and enslaving women for profit was to set up 'roadhouses' in outlying districts, to take advantage of the increased public mobility afforded by the automobile.

They established their first suburban vice outlet in Burnham, on the Illinois-Indiana border. John Patton, elected mayor of that municipality before he was 20, had been a bartender up to that point, getting his start in the saloon trade at the age of 14. He proved an easy man to influence, and soon, Colosimo and Torrio opened their first brothel in the suburbs.

Johnny Torrio was a moderate man in his private life, despite the fact that he was a monstrosity that perpetrated and arranged for murders, torturings and abductions every day. He moved more vice operations into Burnham, and opened up operations in Stickney, a small town to the west of Chicago.

Down the block from Colosimo's nightclub, Torrio bought a four-story building in which he installed a saloon and office on the first floor, gambling dens with solid steel doors on the second and third floors, and a brothel on the fourth.

He called the place, located at 2222 South Wabash Avenue, 'The Four Deuces.' In the basement of this already deeply

At right: A view of Chicago in the 1920s. *Below:* Ads for luxury cars, underscoring the 'carefree abandon' of urban life—underworld white slave abductions gave the lie to such notions.

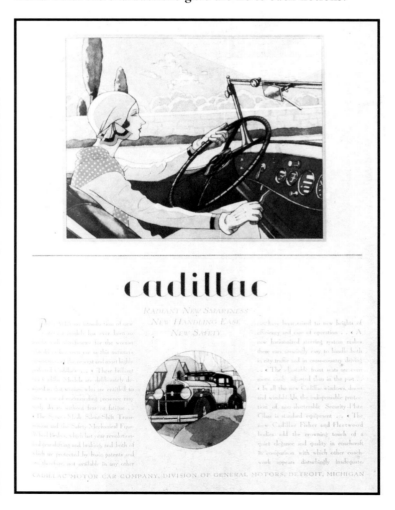

CHICAGO-LOOKING NORTH ON MICHIGAN AVE.
FROM WACKER DRIVE

sinister place, was a torture room where they extracted information from members of rival gangs, killed them, and dispatched their bodies through a tunnel to the rear for a ride via motorcar to 'dumping' sites.

It was 1920, and Torrio, settled in with a big piece of the Colosimo action, sent for his protege, Alphonse Capone. At first he had him working as a bouncer at a brothel that was built directly on the Illinois/Indiana border. When the authorities came to raid, the occupants would run to the other side of the house, thus escaping prosecution. It is assumed that this is where Capone was infected with his eventually fatal case of syphilis.

Torrio soon moved Capone into the Four Deuces, and employed him as a bodyguard, chauffeur, bartender and sidewalk hawker for the fourth-floor brothel. Subhumans themselves, Colosimo and Torrio felt that the girls they ruined were simply commodities, much like the flesh marketeers of today. When the girls were worn out, they 'got rid of them.' Colosimo's own days were numbered, however. Gangsters can very rarely trust any emotional vulnerability in their fellows. One day 'Big Jim' fell passionately in love with a singer in his floor show.

Her name was Dale Winters, and she had operatic ambitions. Big Jim enrolled her in the Chicago Musical College, and badgered Chicago immigrant Enrico Caruso to say nice things about Dale's voice. Colosimo, already married, left his wife and moved in with Dale. He even took up horseback riding at Dale's behest. Colosimo's emotional whirl was an opportunity for Torrio to take over: Torrio had, for at least a year, been sure of his intended direction. On 27 October 1919, Congress had effectively inaugurated the Prohibition Era. On 17 January 1920, Prohibition had taken effect.

Torrio was convinced that the gates to untold wealth through bootlegging were now open, but Colosimo would not move on Torrio's repeated promptings, and their bootlegging was mainly by way of buying illegal booze from others, for use in the nightclubs and roadhouses. There were only 134 Prohibition agents assigned to a the vast midwestern region surrounding Chicago, and 'Big Bill' Thompson had, through an enormous graft campaign that drained the city treasury, won a second term.

The situation whetted Torrio's appetite. Despite his calm exterior, he was a voracious man, and his passion for conquest could no longer be contained. On 11 May 1920, he called Colosimo to inspect a shipment of whiskey at Colosimo's Cafe.

Colosimo grudgingly went to the club at the appointed hour, and finding from his secretary, Frank Camilla, that the shipment had not yet arrived, made a phone call from his office. He then strode away through the club, apparently to meet the shipment—if it came—outside. New Yorker Frankie Yale, hired for the murder by Torrio, shot Colosimo in the back of the head as he strode through the vestibule en route to the door.

At the time, the slaying was a mystery, even though Yale was picked up the next day as he attempted to board an eastbound train home. A porter who had seen the assailant refused to testify against him, and the case was dismissed. At the funeral, the biggest floral wreath was emblazoned with the words 'From Johnny.'

By late 1921, Torrio was expanding his suburban operations, and with gang member Mike 'de Pike' Heitler managing operations, he installed casinos, brothels and roadhouses in formerly law-abiding communities stretching

from Chicago Heights, south of Chicago, to Cicero to the west. They did it all by intimidation and corruption: a few dollars here, a completely bald threat there—and they pinned communities down like experimental rats, injecting them with their very special form of disease.

Harry Guzik and his wife Alma ran the Roamer Inn, in the hamlet of Posen. They obtained their 'recruits' by means of an advertisement for a maid. Of course, once the girl answered, she was never seen again, except by the patrons of the brothel. One of these girls managed to get word of her plight to her family. Her brothers came and rescued her, but after four months under the Guziks' ministrations, she was a mental and physical wreck.

Harry and Alma Guzik were arrested, tried and convicted. They turned to Torrio for help while their case was under appeal: he would have to test his political connections to the maximum. He had in his organization a gunman who was considered the most lethal in Chicago, but it was not for this man's weapons skills that Torrio tapped him this time. The gunsel, Walter Stevens, had political connections in his own right.

It seems that Governor Len Small was under indictment in 1921 for embezzling $600,000 as state treasurer. Stevens and several other underworld figures intimidated and bribed the jury, and got Small acquitted. Small then showed his appreciation to Stevens by helping the Guziks 'beat the rap.' Before the state appeals court handed down its decision, he pardoned the Guziks, and they returned immediately to their brothel operations.

Now secure and assured of the political 'pull' of his gang, Torrio moved into the bootlegging racket full force. At the same time, Al Capone, also known as 'Al Brown,' was rising in prominence within the mob. Torrio found that Capone's abilities complimented his own. Above all else, Capone could be trusted to do a job, when and how he was told to do it: Al was unfortunately good at being a gangster.

Torrio made Capone the manager of the Four Deuces, and cut him in for a 25 percent share of all roadhouse earnings; further, he promised Capone 50 percent of all bootlegging profits. They were now full partners.

Capone's father had died in November, 1920. In true Italian style, he desired to bring his mother and brothers out to Chicago, so that he could take care of them. With his mob 'promotion,' he could now afford to. All but his mother and college-educated brother Matt became involved with gang activity, although only brother, Ralph, joined Al at the command level of the gang.

Capone had a massive, two-story red brick house built on quiet, tree shaded South Prairie Avenue. The house had both luxurious appointments and had a basement that was bullet- and bomb-proof—no doubt built for the eventuality of all-out gang war. Al moved his mother, two sisters, wife and son into the first floor, while bother Ralph and his wife and two children moved into the second floor.

Torrio and Capone could not further expand their enterprises unless they were to forge alliances with the formidable gangland opposition: Dion O'Banion and his gang; the 'Terrible Gennas'; the O'Donnell Gangs and others who were also eager to reap profit from dealing in illegal alcohol.

Dion O'Banion, their main competitor, had been adjudged a psychopathic killer in an early scrape with the

Opposite: **Wyoming militia and confiscated stills in the 1920s. Rural bootleggers supplied much 'product' to urban gangs. Booze and luxury items (see *below*) lured many of the unwary to the city.**

law, and he displayed the same sort of schizophrenic contradictions that many underworld figures did. While he was personally accountable for 27 murders, he felt nothing at all contradictory in his devotion to the very church that utterly condemned his actions. True, the church believes in forgiveness, but only with repentance; and in O'Banion, there was no parting with his murderous ways.

He controlled Chicago's Irish vote, just as Colosimo had controlled Chicago's Italian vote. He was known as 'Chicago's Arch-Criminal,' and yet was unopposed by the law. He was too 'politically useful' to convict, and never spent a day in jail, not even for the many murders that he had committed. His reign at the head of his criminal empire was unruffled, save by the increasing prominence of Colosimo's 'imports' from New York, the upstarts Torrio and Capone.

O'Banion had a sweet Irish tenor, and could be as maudlin as the best; he also loved flowers, and had a flower shop, from which he operated as 'florist to the mobs': whenever a gangster was killed, no matter who had killed him (even if O'Banion had done the job himself), all of gangland Chicago—including O'Banion's bitter enemies—came to his shop for funeral wreaths and bouquets. In fact, it was considered bad taste to order flowers from anyone *but* O'Banion for a funeral.

All his 'patrons' had to do was to show up with the money for the flowers, or call and indicate how much they wanted to spend if they wanted something 'special.' The grandiosity of the funeral display depended on the generally acknowledged rank within the criminal hierarchy of the deceased.

O'Banion also carried three pistols—two under the arms, and one in front, so that he could reach a pistol in any situation. He dressed formally, and insisted that the members of his gang use restraint in public, and put on a show of politesse that would have done credit to an actual gentleman. But O'Banion was also ever ready to use his guns, and he was literally liable to shoot a man for 'looking at him the wrong way.'

He and his right-hand man, Earl 'Hymie' Weiss (who changed his name from the original Polish, Wajiechowski), were committed but very clumsy safe crackers—at one time blowing the entire side off a building without getting the safe open. Weiss is said to have invented 'the one way ride,' which eventually became a favorite mobster practice—a victim was taken to a secluded spot, where he was killed and his body disposed of.

Other O'Banion Gang members were Vincent 'Schemer' Drucci, so named for his imaginative but impractical schemes for committing crimes; George 'Bugs' Moran, a Pole from Minnesota who was an 'enforcer'; and Louis 'Louie Alterie' Varain, O'Banion's chief bodyguard, and a specialist at setting up killings from ambush.

Also, there were the two completely unrelated O'Donnell gangs—the 'West Side O'Donnells' and the 'South Side O'Donnells.' The West Side O'Donnells were led by William 'Klondike' O'Donnell and his brothers Myles and Bernard. The South Side O'Donnells were Edward 'Spike' O'Donnell and brothers Steve, Walter and Tommy.

The West Side O'Donnells were Irish through and through, and hated the Italian and partly Italian gangs, especially newcomers like Torrio and Capone. The South Side O'Donnells never made a move without gangleader Spike, who was, in the early 1920s, serving a sentence for a daylight robbery of a savings bank. While Spike was serving time, his gang found 'employment' with Torrio and Capone, doing odd jobs for their mob. Seemingly immobilized, the South Side O'Donnells were scheming for the day when Spike would be released, and would once more lead them.

In 'Little Italy,' the most fearsome opposition were the 'Terrible Gennas.' The Genna brothers, Sam, Jim, Pete, Angelo, Tony and Mike, had been on the streets since childhood, their parents having died young. They stayed together and swiftly built up a bankroll through Black Hand extortion. Through paying off ward bosses, they entrenched themselves in illegal gambling, moonshining, political terrorism for hire and extortion.

Their moonshine operation included the biggest bootleg alcohol plant in Chicago, and a multitude of 'home stills' that they forced the dwellers of various tenements to keep going in their kitchens. In addition, they paid minimal sums for flunkies to stand by and tend the stills. Their biggest profit came from the conversion of wood alcohol into a barely potable beverage that left its imbibers with racking pains in their bodies for days after. Yet, because it was so cheap, it sold unbelievably well.

Sam was the chief organizer; Jim and Pete were the moonshining technicians; Angelo and Mike were the killers and enforcers; and Tony was the *consigliere*, or strategist, who plotted what moves they would make and when. Unlike his fat, uncultured brothers, Tony was a slender aesthete of sorts who loved 'higher culture.' It added a polish to his gangsterish demeanor.

The Gennas, Sicilians themselves, recruited Sicilian bodyguards and Sicilian strong arm men. Among these, Samuzzo 'Samoots' Amatuna was a foppish triggerman who once killed a laundry wagon horse because the laundry had scorched one of his shirts; Orazio 'the Scourge' Tropea specialized in squeezing the pennies out of poor Sicilian immigrants; he also superstitiously believed that he was a sorcerer of sorts, with the power of 'the evil eye'; Giuseppe Nerone, an ex-mathematics teacher who fled from the law in Sicily, was a killer; John Scalise and Albert Anselmi had likewise fled the Sicilian authorities, and were professional killers.

Over on the West Side of town was the Druggan-Lake Gang. Never large in numbers, the gang pre-existed the two leaders, Terry Druggan and Frank Lake, and had been in operation as a virtual 'college of criminality' since the turn of the century. Druggan, Lake and associates specialized in burglary. With Prohibition, they moved to buy into as many breweries as possible, and hijacked a good many bootleg beer cargoes as well.

Another small gang was the Saltis-McErlane Gang. Joe 'the Pollock' Saltis was a bootlegger whose subhuman brutality was such that he bludgeoned a woman merchant to death because she wouldn't turn her ice cream parlor into an outlet for his booze. His partner, Frank McErlane, was a compulsive killer. When drunk, he was doubly dangerous. On a binge, he once shot a man in the head just to prove his marksmanship. He then raced the police to the state line, and by the time extradition had been effected, the 'only witness' to his crime had been savagely slain with an axe.

Then, there were Ragen's Colts, a former athletic club led by a charismatic man named Frank Ragen. As Ragen's political fortunes rose, so too did Ragen's Colts, numbering in the hundreds. Over the years, thanks to Ragen's connections, the Colts turned out aldermen, police chiefs, county trea-

surers and other political personages, as well as a number of well-protected racketeers. Ralph Sheldon was a notable example of the latter. With Prohibition, the Ralph Sheldon wing of Ragen's Colts went heavily into bootlegging.

At the outset of Prohibition, brewers were faced with closing up shop or converting their equipment to make legal 'near beer' of one-half percent alcoholic content. Some chose neither option, and fell into partnerships with mobsters, supplying the equipment and expertise to make bootleg products, while the gangsters provided protection, transportation, marketing and legal liability.

Torrio found a brewer, Joseph Stenson, who was already doing business with Frank Lake and Terry Druggan. Torrio became another of the brewer's partners, on the condition that he and Capone could operate four breweries.

With the potential for big profits and ferocious warfare between competing gangs at hand, it was time for diplomacy: the Torrio/Capone Gang presented their various rivals with a plan for mutual profiteering, talking them into concentrating on bootlegging—a racket with not nearly the risk of robbery, and with many times the potential for profit. The idea was to provide a cohesive, city-wide organization without violating already-established territories of operation.

No speakeasy in a given gang's territory would be allowed to buy from a source outside of that gang.

Encroachments and hijackings could be brought to the attention of the other gang leaders, and they would all have a hand in the punishment of the outsider. Torrio would provide all the beer needed at $50 a barrel, but if a gang wanted to manufacture their own beer or whiskey, they were free to

Above left: 'Bootlegging': small amounts of illegal alcohol were often transported in this way. *Above:* Mr and Mrs Dion O'Banion. O'Banion was 'Chicago's Arch-Criminal,' and gangland's florist.

do so. Torrio also offered his well-known services as a facilitator, and would arbitrate disputes between rival gangs where an infraction of the aforesaid 'rules' was in question.

Torrio and O'Banion agreed to trade commodities: O'Banion's smuggled Canadian whiskey for Torrio's beer; in exchange for guaranteed protection of their alcohol stills in Little Italy, the Gennas guaranteed safe passage for Torrio's beer trucks through Genna territory. And so on and so forth—until Spike O'Donnell, of the South Side O'Donnells, came home from prison.

With the help of a killer from New York, Harry Hasmiller, the South Side O'Donnells launched an assault against the Torrio/Capone and Saltis/McErlane gangs. O'Donnell 'salesmen' George 'Sport' Bucher and George Meeghan threatened the bartenders in both territories with dire injury unless they bought the O'Donnells' hijacked goods.

On 7 September 1923, Bucher and Meeghan—accompanied by Steve, Walter and Tommy O'Donnell, and a friend of Spike's from prison, Jerry O'Conner—went on a frenzy of intimidation deep in Saltis/McErlane territory. Unbeknownst to them, Frank McErlane and several of his thugs were stalking them. The O'Donnell Gang finished their evening of clubbing and furniture smashing, and were relaxing in a 'friendly' saloon on South Street when McErlane and company burst in upon them, guns drawn. In the melee that ensued, all the O'Donnell bunch escaped, except for Jerry O'Conner, who was killed by a blast from McErlane's shotgun.

On the 17th of that month, Bucher and Meeghan were driving two truckloads of beer along a stretch of highway south of Chicago. McErlane and his favorite gunman, Danny McFall, waylaid and killed them with shotguns. On the same highway, just one month later, O'Donnell beer convoy drivers William 'Shorty' Egan and Morrie Keane were way-

laid and taken for the proverbial 'ride' by Frank McErlane and a man identified as gunman Walter Stevens. Keane was killed, and Egan, surprisingly, survived severe shotgun wounds. Another driver, Phil Corrigan, perished in like manner not long after.

Walter O'Donnell and Harry Hasmiller were killed, not long afterward, in a running gun battle with Saltis-McErlane forces. While indictments were handed down for some of the killings, every charge was *nolle prossed*. A new figure was beginning to appear in Chicago police reports, too: several witnesses had seen 'Al Brown,' also known as Al Capone, at the scene of some of the shootings, but no one could really *prove* anything, could they?

With the accession of Judge William E Dever to the mayoralty of Chicago, the spirit of reform was upon Chicago once again. 'Big Bill' Thompson had been so openly corrupt that he and his henchmen made no bones about bilking the public, and while draining the city treasuries, his campaign manager Fred Lundin said, 'To hell with the public! We're at the trough and we're going to feed!' Dever, at least (and at last!) an honest man, was a 'shoo-in' for election in 1923. Torrio, Capone and their gang saw Cicero as a relatively 'open' town where their enterprises could flourish.

Things looked bad for the vice rackets in Chicago: the mobsters concentrated on building up their empires in the suburbs. The politically corrupt suburb of Cicero was run by slot machine racketeer Eddie Vogel, who essentially gave orders to the mayor, Joseph Klenha. The West Side O'Donnells already had a stake in Cicero—they were the dominant peddlers of booze there—and Eddie Tancl, an ex-boxer with mob connections, had a controlling share of Cicero's political machinery, too.

Torrio set up a brothel in Cicero, only to see it shut down by the police under Vogel's command. He set up another,

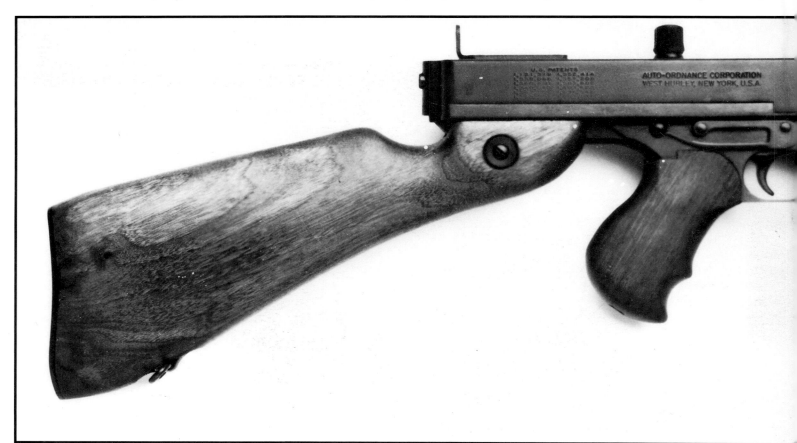

with the same result. Torrio had known in advance that this would be the case: he simply wanted to set up a forum for bargaining. After the second shutdown, he used his influence with the Cook County Sheriff's Department, and had Vogel's slot machines confiscated.

Vogel was then ready to bargain. In a conference with the West Side O'Donnells, Torrio and Vogel, an agreement was struck whereby Vogel was guaranteed protection for his slot machine operations; the O'Donnells were guaranteed their territory; and Torrio was guaranteed a share in bootlegging in Cicero, outside of the O'Donnell territory there.

Torrio was also given the 'right' to set up gambling houses in Cicero, and to establish a base for all other operations except for prostitution. Tancl, on the other hand, openly asserted his hatred of Torrio.

Meanwhile, things were 'heating up' in Chicago. Mayor Dever appointed the hard-working Morgan A Collins as Chief of Police, and the two set to work trying to break the rackets. Heavy inroads were made into vice, gambling and bootlegging: for once, the city seemed to be going straight. While the rackets were not completely uprooted, they were severely hampered. In answer to Torrio's attempt to bribe him, Collins padlocked the Four Deuces. Torrio decided to take a vacation to Italy, fearing possible arrest.

He left Al Capone in charge. Capone, still maintaining his residence in Chicago, took as his gang headquarters the Hawthorne Inn at 4833 22nd Street, in Cicero. He had this two-story brick building reinforced and bullet-proofed. The 1924 elections in Cicero were cause for concern—perhaps the same spirit of reform would strike Cicero if the incumbent, Joe Klenha, lost.

Both sides imported gangster troops from Chicago to 'insure' their candidate's election. Thugs stood over the voters and snatched ballots from their hands if their answers to probing question were 'the wrong ones.' The ballots were then re-marked and handed back to the 'errant' voters, and under threat of being shot, they were forced to put the remarked ballots in the box.

A group of concerned Ciceronians called for help, and detachments of Chicago police arrived: gun battles erupted between gangsters and police. Al and Frank Capone, and their cousin Charlie Fischetti, were accosted as they intimidated voters at a polling place. They elected to shoot it out, and Frank Capone was slain by a police shotgun blast. Al and Charlie fled the scene. Fischetti was arrested but was released immediately, and no charges were pressed.

Frank's funeral was even more lavish than had been Big Jim Colosimo's, with so many bouquets and wreaths that some of them had to be hung on the trees and bushes outside of Al's house, where Frank was laid out for viewing. In yet another defeat for justice, Klenha won re-election by a landslide. Shortly after this, the Hawthorne Smoke Shop, next door to the Hawthorne Inn, became the nerve center for a network of gambling 'dives.' The Hawthorne Smoke Shop itself made as much as $50,000 per day, in its around-the-clock operations.

Torrio returned from his 'vacation' in 1924. With the Four Deuces padlocked and Torrio back in town, the Capone/Torrio Gang set up a new 'main headquarters' at 2146 South Michigan Avenue, where Jake Guzik's bookkeeping ledgers were kept. In spring of 1924, a raid on the new headquarters by the Chicago police put these ledgers into the hands of crusading Mayor Dever. But, before anything could be done with them, a Torrio pawn, Judge Howard Hayes, impounded the ledgers and restored them to Torrio.

Chicago became known for drive-by shootings with the .45 caliber Thompson (below) and the wide-window sedan (at bottom).

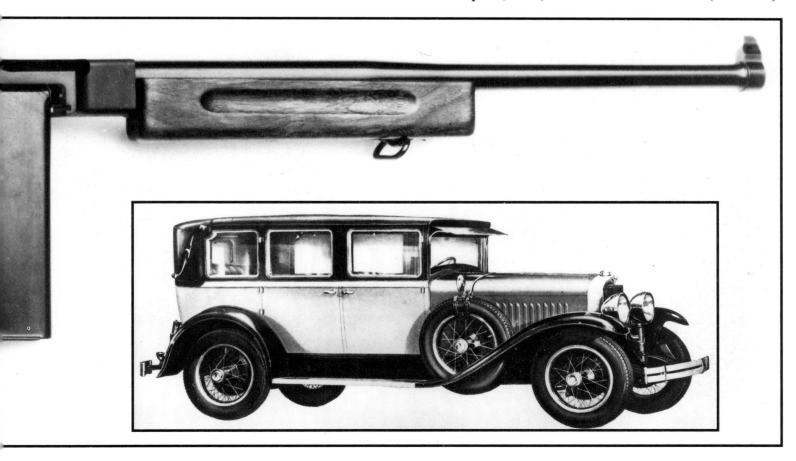

Capone was soon arrested for a murder he committed on 8 May 1924, while ostensibly avenging an insult to his bookkeeper Jake Guzik. After going underground for a few days, Capone resurfaced at a Chicago police station. Interrogated for hours by prosecutor William H McSwiggin, he baldly lied, saying he didn't know Torrio, Guzik or Joe Howard, the man he murdered. In addition, the witnesses who had seen the incident changed their testimony, having been threatened by the mob.

That same year, Eddie Tancl was assassinated by Myles O'Donnell and his sidekick Jim Doherty. In a spectacular shootout that left O'Donnell unconscious with four bullet wounds, Doherty nearly incoherent with severe injuries and Tancl himself dead, another chapter of violence was written in the misbegotten annals of gang-era Cicero.

Dion O'Banion and the Gennas were also creating friction. The Gennas had invaded O'Banion's territory with their rotgut whiskey, and O'Banion remonstrated with Torrio about the situation. Torrio was loathe to differ with fellow Sicilians on the part of an Irishman, so O'Banion hijacked a $30,000 shipment of Genna moonshine.

As if May, 1924 weren't already eventful enough, O'Banion approached Torrio and Capone in mid-month, saying that he feared the Gennas and was going to retire, and wanted to sell them his share in the Sieben Brewery. Upon payment of $500,000 for his share, O'Banion offered to help the Italians with moving a shipment as a good will gesture. On 19 May 1924, a 13-truck shipment of beer was ready to roll from the brewery, and O'Banion, 'Hymie' Weiss, Louie Alterie, Torrio and 22 of Torrio's best drivers were on hand, only to be raided by a large contingent of Chicago policemen, led by Chief Collins.

Torrio paid his bail and found out that O'Banion had set them up as an act of revenge, for he hated Torrio and Capone's incursions on his former supremacy in gangland Chicago. O'Banion was heard shortly after, bragging about the way he'd 'rubbed that pimp's nose in the mud.'

The Gennas had been forbidden by Mike Merlo, president of the Chicago Chapter of the Unione Siciliane, to kill O'Banion. Now, however, Merlo lay dying of cancer, and O'Banion was 'fair game.' When Merlo did die, Dion O'Banion was, of course, the florist for the funeral. Jim Genna and Carmen

Below and at right: Edward G Robinson in the 1931 First National-Vitaphone motion picture *Little Caesar*—emulated by many later gangster films. Mobsters were widely notorious.

Vacco (a city appointee who owed much to Merlo's influence) stopped by O'Banion's shop on 9 November, to make sure that he would be open late that night: more of Merlo's friends would be stopping by to give him orders for wreaths and flowers.

The next day, O'Banion was still busy filling orders, and none of his helpers, save William Crutchfield, his porter, were yet at work, having stayed late the night before. Three men came by, and the porter heard O'Banion say 'Hello, boys, you want Merlo's flowers?' As he reached forth to shake hands, one of the men grabbed his hand, and the other executioners pinioned O'Banion's other arm, making access to any of his 'trademark' three guns impossible. The men then simply shot him numerous times and fled.

This occasioned the second huge gangster funeral within a week, and tens of thousands lined the streets to view the preposterously overblown funeral cortege. O'Banion, the gangster churchgoer, was not given a church funeral, as he had never repented of his deeds. Buried among a million flowers in unconsecrated ground, Dion O'Banion was dead.

'Hymie' Weiss then assumed leadership of O'Banion's gang. An inquest returned no arrest warrants, but it was widely believed that the murderers were probably Frankie Yale, in from New York; John Scalise and Albert Anselmi—and, that they had been set to work by Johnny Torrio, Al Capone and the Gennas.

On 12 January 1925, 'Hymie' Weiss, 'Schemer' Drucci and Bugs Moran nearly killed two of Capone's bodyguards and severely wounded his chauffeur, when they perpetrated a drive-by shooting at State and 55th Streets. They had missed Capone himself by minutes, but succeeded in destroying his car with gunfire.

This led him to buy a custom-ordered, seven-ton, armor plated Cadillac limousine with half-inch bulletproof glass. In addition, Capone took to travelling with a car in front and a car behind, both full of his henchmen. He seldom ever again walked outside without a retinue of bodyguards—two deep in front, back and on both sides. He constantly changed times and dates of meetings at the last moment, to foil assassination attempts.

Even with these precautions, Capone's new chauffeur, Tommy Cuiringione, was kidnapped and killed by Weiss and his gang.

Johnny Torrio, meanwhile had been on another 'vacation,'

and returned to the sure knowledge that he would be as much a marked man as Capone. He sought sanctuary, and pled guilty on 23 January 1925, while on trial for the Sieben Brewery escapade: in prison, perhaps O'Banion's gangland heirs could not reach him. The judge gave Torrio five days to settle his affairs.

On 24 January 24, Torrio and his wife were returning from a shopping trip: Weiss gunmen ambushed him as he stepped from his limousine to the street: shot in the jaw, chest, arm and groin, he was spared the usual *coup de grace* shot to the head when the thug trying to administer it found his weapon empty. The attackers fled. At the hospital, Torrio admitted knowing all four of his would-be killers, by refused to identify them. However, police were sure that Bugs Moran was one of them—but an indictment was never returned.

Torrio left the hospital in three weeks, and was sentenced to nine months at Lake County Jail in Waukegan, Illinois. His cell was closely guarded, and had bullet proof glass windows. Torrio was allowed to carry on 'business conferences' at the jail. In March, he had a conference with Capone and their lawyers: he had decided to retire, and transferred all of his gangland assets to Capone. When he was released, he took up a position in New York as teacher and gangland 'gray eminence' to the notorious Lucky Luciano, who was, in the early 1930s, to become the most powerful gangster in America.

It was at about this time that Al adopted the nickname 'Snorky,' which was slang for 'opulent,' and was meant to convey that Al Capone was a man of the world, indeed. With Torrio's decision, Capone became 'the boss' in Chicago. Of course, the warfare had made all of the inter-gang agreements useless.

The gangs now tended to align themselves ethnically, with the Irish, Poles and Jews backing up Hymie Weiss and company, and the Italians tending to stay with Capone.

Angelo Genna had become president of the local chapter of the Unione Siciliane upon former President Merlo's death. Capone removed the gang's headquarters to Chicago's Hotel Metropole on 2300 South Michigan Avenue, not far from the Four Deuces, and not far from the Genna's territory.

Capone and his enemies would soon make Chicago such a battleground that even the most corrupt police forces had to act against gangsters, due to the 'bad public relations' generated by the warfare in Chicago and its suburbs. Capone shored up the organization he had inherited from Torrio, correctly anticipating a vicious struggle in his attempt to establish dominion of the cesspool that was Chicago's underworld.

The personnel of the soon-to-be notorious 'Capone Gang' was as follows: Jake Guzik was the accountant and business manager; Frank 'The Enforcer' Nitti was 'promoted' from killer to treasurer and liaison to the Unione Siciliane; Ralph 'Bottles' Capone was director of liquor sales, being violently efficient at persuading saloon keepers to 'buy his brand'; Charlie Fischetti had become, with Lawrence Mangano, co-director of liquor distribution; Frank Pope was the chief horseplaying bookie; Peter Penovich was in charge of other gambling operations; Hymie 'Loudmouth' Levine was chief collector for gambling operations that were not wholly owned by Capone; Mike 'de Pike' Heitler and Harry Guzik ran the brothels; and Tony Lombardo was Capone's *consigliere*, or chief advisor.

Louis Cowan was the mob's bail bondsman, and operated, for sentimental reasons, from a newspaper stand at 25th Street and 52nd Avenue—a call to a nearby phone booth would cause him to scurry across the sidewalk to his huge limousine, which would whisk away him to aid any gang affiliate in trouble with the law. James 'Bomber' Belcastro was the head of the mob's demolition squad, an adjunct to their 'enforcement' and sales offices; Phil D'Andrea was Capone's chief bodyguard; William 'Three-Fingered Jack' White and Sam 'Golf Bag' Hunt filled the vacuum left by Fischetti's and Nitti's promotions, and were the mob's chief killers—Hunt preferred carrying his weapons in his eponymous golf bag.

Antonino 'Joe Batters' Accardo, Felice Lucia (also known as 'Paul the Waiter' Ricca), Sam 'Mooney' Giancana and Murray 'The Camel' Humphries were still more of Capone's underlings and thugs, specializing in bludgeonings, shootings, mutilations, murders and other acts associated with extortion and robbery.

'Machine Gun' Jack McGurn was Capone's favorite killer. He was born Vincenzo de Mora, and had unsuccessfully been a prizefighter in his youth. He was nicknamed for his favorite weapon, and fancied himself a ladies' man, being a dapper dresser with a 'Rudolph Valentino' hairstyle featuring heavy use of pomade. Whenever he killed someone, he left a nickel clutched in the victim's hand.

There were many, many more minions under Capone's

Below: Hotel Metropole, on South Michigan Avenue—Capone's new headquarters in 1925. *At right:* Paul Muni, in the title role of the 1932 movie *Scarface*, which mirrored Chicago's violent years.

power, and these were a wide assortment of safe crackers, muggers, pimps, flunkies and general ne'er-do-wells who sought 'a piece of the action.' Altogether, Capone's organization was an army that would be involved in some of the bloodiest gang warfare ever witnessed.

The new phase of Chicago bloodshed began on 25 May 1925, when Weiss, Moran and Drucci ambushed Angelo Genna, who was en route to paying, in cash, for a suburban bungalo in which to set up housekeeping with his bride of one month. Genna, driving a sporty roadster, outran the Weiss gangsters, until he misjudged a corner and smashed into a lamppost. His pursuers killed him as he sat, helplessly trapped in the wreckage.

A few weeks later, Weiss and gang approached 'Samoots' Amatuna and promised to treat him lavishly if he would set up Scalise and Anselmi for them. Amatuna pretended to agree—and then informed the rest of the Genna Gang, who promptly came up with a scheme that would put Weiss, *et al* in *their* gunsights. The time agreed upon between Amatuna and Weiss was the morning of 13 June at nine o'clock.

As Weiss mobsters Moran and Drucci sat in their car—ready to riddle Scalise and Anselmi when Amatuna paraded them past their gunsights—Scalise, Anselmi and Mike Genna drove past them and opened up with shotguns.

The attackers were seen in flight by a carful of detectives, who immediately gave chase. No better driver than his brother Angelo had been, Mike Genna swerved to miss a lumber truck and crashed the car. Detectives Michael Conway, Harold Olson, William Sweeney and Charles Walsh confronted the mobsters, who blasted them with a barrage of shotgun fire. Conway was badly wounded; Olson and Walsh were killed. Sweeney, protected by the hood of his police car, traded shots with the mobsters.

At the sound of the gunfire, factory workers poured forth from the mills in the neighborhood, and the mobsters fled, with Sweeney in pursuit. Scalise and Anselmi escaped down an alley, and Mike Genna was wounded in the leg, the bullet severing his femoral artery. Bleeding copiously, he collapsed in a warehouse, where he was found shortly thereafter, only to bleed to death in the ambulance *en route* to the hospital.

Scalise and Anselmi lost their hats in escaping the scene, and demonstrated their gangsterish lack of perspective when they dashed into a hat shop to buy new ones. The hat shop owner grew suspicious at the excited pair and hailed a passing police car. The two were charged with first degree murder, one count for each of Sweeney's fellow officers.

Badly wounded but not killed in the drive-by shooting, Moran and Drucci spent weeks in the hospital recuperating, and would return to do battle with renewed vengeance.

The deaths of Angelo and Mike Genna opened access to the presidency of the Unione Siciliane for Capone's mob. A Neapolitan himself, Al could never fill that post, but his *consigliere*, Tony Lombardo could. If he succeeded in installing Lombardo, then the fealty of Sicilian-dominated Little Italy would pass from the Gennas and their minions to 'Snorky' Capone. Still, there were a few Gennas in the way—including Tony Genna and gang lieutenant Samoots Amatuna, both likely prospects for the post.

Ironically, Weiss inadvertently helped Capone by having Genna killed. On 8 July, Giuseppe Nerone, ostensibly a friend of the Genna Gang, called Tony Genna for a meeting about 'important information.' In front of Cutilla's Grocery on Grand Avenue, Nerone grasped Genna's extended hand,

and as a second killer pumped five shots into his back, Tony Genna died in much the same way as did Dion O'Banion. Shortly thereafter, Nerone himself was slain in a barber shop, effectively sealing the case.

The remaining Gennas fled Chicago in panic, only returning years later to do business as importers of cheese and olive oil. Under the direction of Samoots Amatuna, the defense fund for Scalise and Anselmi was built by the usual means: extortion. With the help of Orazio 'The Scourge' Tropea and Ecola 'The Eagle' Baldelli, the survivors of the Genna Gang raised $50,000.

Almost as a sidelight to all this carnage, the Saltis-McErlane/South Side O'Donnells war was also brought to a conclusion. On 25 September 1925, McErlane became the first mobster to use a Thompson submachine gun. His target was Spike O'Donnell, loitering of an evening on the corner of 63rd and Western Avenue. Cruising past, in a style that was to become a hallmark of gangland stupidity, McErlane riddled the storefront against which O'Donnell was standing, but, due to his lack of practice with the new weapon, every one of McErlane's shots went wild.

The next month, near the same spot, Spike and brother Tommy were sitting in Spike's car when McErlane machine gunned them in a similar drive-by attack. Tommy O'Donnell was wounded, but Spike was again unscathed. He left Chicago, however, and did not return for two years.

The trial for the killing of Detective Olson began on 5 October. The prosecution's star witness, Detective Sweeney, lost his home to a gangland bomber on 11 October, while jury selection was in process. Sweeney and other elements of the prosecution had been receiving threats by phone and through the mails all summer. So many jurors were threatened that it took three weeks to select a jury.

When the trial commenced, Scalise and Anselmi were identified by dozens of witnesses, but the defense, led by Michael Ahern, Capone's favorite legal pawn, broke new legal ground: Ahern said, 'If a policeman detains you, even for a moment, against your will [and you kill him], you are not guilty of murder, but only manslaughter. If the policeman uses force of arms, you may kill him in self-defense and emerge from the law unscathed.'

Incredibly, it worked. Scalise and Anselmi were found guilty of manslaughter, and received 14 years in the penitentiary, but the resulting outrage of both police and public led the judge to move up the date of the trial for the death of Detective Walsh. Meanwhile, the Weiss Gang and the West Side O'Donnell Gang, combining forces to prevent a resurrection of the decimated Genna Gang, targeted Samoots Amatuna—who had just been made President of the Unione Siciliane—as the logical new leader of the Genna Gang. On the evening of 13 November 1925, Weiss/O'Donnell gunmen slew Amatuna as he sat in a Cicero barbershop.

Soon, Capone got his wish, and Tony Lombardo was installed as President of the Chicago Chapter of the Unione Siciliane. Capone now had 'clout' in Sicilian-dominated Little Italy.

Three days after the death of Samoots Amatuna, on his way home from the funeral, gunman Eddy Zion was ambushed and killed; two weeks after that, another mobster, Bummy Goldstein, was slain by shotgun as he stood at the counter of a drugstore. Both were members of the gangs that killed Amatuna.

By this time, Torrio had gotten out of prison. He boarded a

train under heavy mob protection, and met his wife in New York. After a conference with the notorious Charlie 'Lucky' Luciano, Torrio and his wife sailed for Italy. Torrio was, however, forced by anti-mob dictator Benito Mussolini to return to Manhattan, where he acted as an underworld mentor to Luciano.

Capone, his wife Mae and son Al, Jr, went to Manhattan as well, to have an emergency operation performed on 'Sonny's' mastoid gland. While there, on Christmas Eve, Capone paid a visit to one of his early haunts, the Adonis Social Club. At the bar were several irascible Irishmen, Richard 'Peg Leg' Lonergan, Aaron Harms, Cornelius 'Needles' Ferry, James Hart, Joseph 'Ragtime' Howard and Patrick 'Happy' Maloney.

Lonergan was the leader of this informal but notorious gang, and his presence in the Adonis—an Italian hangout— was seen as a direct affront. Not only that, but he and his men were loudly insulting of the regular customers (none of whom were the average law-abiding citizens). Capone had come in at about two in the morning with several companions. As soon as he and his men sat at a table in the back of the saloon, someone turned the lights out and the place erupted in gunfire.

Lonergan, Harms and Ferry had all died of shots to the head; Hart was shot in the legs, and refused to identify his assailants, or even admit that he'd been in the Adonis Social Club that night. No other witnesses came forth. The case was dismissed. Capone was not yet so widely known that he was a 'public figure' beyond Chicago and its suburbs: a New York police reporter identified him as 'a doorman at the club,' an error that made his old associate Lucky Luciano roar with laughter.

His boy's surgery a success, Capone and family returned to Chicago in time for another bloodbath. During the 'collection efforts' for the second Scalise-Anselmi trial, Henry Spingola, Angelo Genna's brother-in-law and a heavy contributor to the first trail, refused to shell out more. On his way home from refusing to pay collector Orazio 'The Scourge' Tropea, he was ambushed and slain by shotgun fire.

Agostino and Antonio Morici, purveyors of yeast and sugar to Little Italy's moonshining industry, having contributed to the first trial like Spingola, also declared that they would give no more. They were also slain by shotgun, in a rare moment without their bodyguards. Relatives and friends retaliated swiftly: on 15 February, Tropea was ambushed by shotgun on Halstead Street; on the 24th of that month, the body of Vito Bascone—an underling of 'the collectors'—was found in a ditch in Stickney, Illinois; Ecola 'The Eagle' Baldelli's mangled body was found that night in a North Chicago alley.

At right: State Street, Chicago, at lunch hour. Some Capone-era mobsters had no qualms about using weapons like the Thompson submachine gun *(below)* on enemies, even in such crowds.

NOON HOUR ON STATE STREET CHICAGO

That very day, the Vice President of the United States, Charles G Dawes, presented a petition to Congress for the immediate commencement of a federal investigation of organized crime in the Chicago area. The petition had been developed by the Better Government Association of Chicago and Cook County, and it spotlighted not only the mobsters, but government officials—from ward bosses, to policemen, to the Illinois State's Attorney, Robert E Crowe, who was notoriously and (and some said 'purposely') ineffective in his role.

Giving added impetus to the federal investigation was the outcome of the second trial of Scalise and Anselmi: it was a travesty as was the first. One juror admitted to the judge that he couldn't bring in a guilty verdict for fear of what would happen to his family. Two witnesses also blatantly lied that the policemen had fired first. The thugs were acquitted, and were remanded to Joliet State Prison to begin serving their 14 years, with time off for good behavior, on the first conviction.

Then, adding even more fuel to the fire, Assistant State's Attorney William H McSwiggin was killed by machine gun on 27 April 1926. He was the victim of a drive-by shooting that also claimed the lives of known mobsters Jim Doherty and Tom Duffy. Myles O'Donnell had escaped injury when

he dropped to the floor of his car, as did his chauffeur, Edward Hanley, an ex-policeman. The group, including McSwiggin, had pulled up in front of the Pony Inn, an underground hangout in Cicero.

At first, the case was cited as one in which McSwiggin was 'trying to obtain information from gang members' and had inadvertently been on the receiving end of a 'hit' meant for the gangsters. McSwiggin had been a sharp and assiduous young prosecutor, and at age 26, had a promising future. State's Attorney Crowe swore that 'It will be war to the hilt with these gangsters!'

Still others skeptically added that they lacked confidence in Crowe, and that such pronouncements of his were often rallying cries to 'do nothing.' Crowe called up a special Grand Jury to investigate the murders, and when the public grew even more skeptical, due to the suspicious ineffectiveness of Crowe Grand Juries in the past, Crowe then called upon State's Attorney General Oscar Carlstrom to head the Grand Jury.

This was yet another ruse: the truth was that Crowe and Carlstrom were up to their necks in the tangled mass of connections tying law enforcement agencies to the bootlegging industry. Carlstrom diverted the Grand Jury's attention to the scandals surrounding the killing of a deputy warden at

Joliet Prison, and filled the headlines with discoveries of a syndicate for the sale of pardons and paroles. This 'investigation' returned not a single indictment.

As of 5 May, there was no evidence in the McSwiggin case. Then, the owner of the Pony Inn, Harry Madigan, revealed that the O'Donnells had been expanding their operations, cutting in on 'Snorky' Capone's bootlegging territory in Cicero. Other witnesses came forth and testified that they had seen Capone and fellow gang members in hurried conversation in a Cicero restaurant; that Capone had gone to a cabinet and pulled out a submachine gun, and that they had all left the restaurant in a group an hour before the killing.

It was determined that Capone's gang had used five cars, bristling with machine guns and shotguns, to trail and then assault the O'Donnell car. Capone rebutted the charges in a local paper by saying that he wouldn't kill McSwiggin—he claimed that he liked him, and that McSwiggin was on his payroll: 'I paid McSwiggin and I paid him plenty, and I got what I was paying for.'

At one point, McSwiggin's father confronted Capone in a saloon, and Capone handed him his pistol, saying, 'If you think I did it, shoot me.' Capone was, again and again, shortly to prove that this was an accurate description of his own code of gangland justice.

Whether it was actually true is a matter of debate, gangsters having had no compunction about lying, and Capone having every reason to smear a man he had every reason to dislike. We may never know, however, as Capone then vanished from sight for four months, only to resurface and reiterate that he could have killed McSwiggin in private, and that he had nothing against the other victims. He was exonerated. Altogether, seven grand juries were convened, with confusing and conflicting testimony, only to 'do nothing' in the end.

Crowe now had to do some actual raiding, or public opinion would lead to his own indictment. He had 100 Chicago detectives deputized for raids into the vice concentrations in the suburbs, heavily damaged nearly 30 Capone 'resorts,' and inflicted a death blow to Capone's newest brothel, located in Forest View. This little town hated the mob from the start, but had been literally taken by force. After the Crowe raiders emptied the brothel, Forest View vigilantes set fire to it, and the local fire department gladly let it burn to the ground.

Below left: The view from the Observation Deck (*below*) of the Board of Trade Building. Capone, Moran and other hoodlums grafted allies in government, and Chicago was at their mercy.

CHICAGO BOARD OF TRADE BLDG. AND OBSERVATORY

Chief raider John Stege confiscated ledger books of mob operations, and most importantly, captured the master ledgers from the Hawthorne Smoke Shop. These were, quite suspiciously, not seen as important at the time—but then again, they weren't returned to the mob, either. They were left to molder with other 'unimportant' material in the State's Attorney's Office for four years. The ledgers would, eventually, provide the very evidence that the federal government needed to tie Al Capone to the enormous profits of his illicit enterprises, and thus indict him for non-payment of income tax.

It was just another coverup for a situation that even the distraught elder McSwiggin refused to comment upon, saying it 'would blow the lid off Chicago' if he did. No one ever found out. Meanwhile, Capone continued to shore up his ambition to be 'king' of the Chicago underworld.

The violence with the Hymie Weiss Gang was wearing on Capone's nerves, and he decided to do something about it. On 10 August 1926, Weiss and Schemer Drucci were en route to the Standard Oil Building at 910 South Michigan Avenue, where they were to pay Trustee of the Chicago Sanitation District Morris Elder and Assistant State's Attorney John Sbarbo (also gangland's favorite undertaker) $13,500 in cash for an undisclosed deal.

At the corner of Michigan and Ninth Streets, three gunmen in a car attempted a drive-by shooting of Weiss and Drucci as they made their way through the bustling lunch hour crowd. Two gunmen jumped from the car and continued firing. Drucci and Weiss returned the fire from their hurriedly found places of concealment.

A police car appeared, and the assassins' car sped off, leaving its two troopers on foot stranded. Drucci jumped up on the runningboard of a civilian's car and told him to 'beat it, fast' but by then was surrounded by policemen. Drucci refused to identify a captured assailant, Capone gunman Louis Barko, even when Barko was brought to him face-to-face. The shooting was one more incident of menace on the streets of Chicago. One man, an office worker, was wounded in the leg.

A week later, Weiss, Drucci and their lawyer were headed for the Standard Oil Building again, but this time, they drove. Near their destination, a car rammed them to the curb and its occupants riddled Weiss' car with a fusillade of bullets. The three miraculously escaped and fled into the shelter of the Standard Oil Building. Again, there were no arrests, and again, the pedestrians of the lunch hour business district had 'something to talk about.'

On the afternoon of 20 September 1926, Al Capone and bodyguard 'Slippery' Frank Rio sat at a table in the Hawthorne Restaurant, anticipating the autumn meet that was to take place at the nearby Hawthorne Race Track. It was a sunny day in Cicero, and the broad boulevard of West 22nd Street sparkled with well-dressed folks who were strolling in the fine weather.

From an approaching car came the concussions of machine gun fire, which were, in fact, blanks meant to bring the patrons of the restaurant—especially 'Snorky' Capone—to the door. Rio grabbed Capone and threw him on the floor, just as the next car in what turned out to be an 11-car caravan let loose with a volley of real machine gun bullets. Fire poured from each of the other cars, as each in turn slowly rolled past the front of the restaurant. When the next to the last car pulled up, it stopped, and, guarded by shot-gunners from the last car, a gunman armed with a Thompson casually walked up to the restaurant doorway, knelt, and emptied a 100-round magazine into the interior.

Three honks came from a car in the caravan, and the gunner and his 'guards' strolled back to their cars, and the caravan proceeded unhurriedly down the street, heading back to Chicago. Hymie Weiss had mounted an unprecedented assault upon Capone territory. Surprisingly, no one was killed, and only two people were wounded—Capone gunman Louis Barko, who was walking into the restaurant as the shooting started, and Mrs Clyde Freeman, a tourist who had been wounded and suffered an eye injury from flying glass. (In a public relations move, Capone paid $5000 for specialists to repair Mrs. Freeman's eye.)

On 11 October, Weiss was tired from having spent the day rigging a jury in the trial of two of his gunmen, Lefty Koncil and Mitters Foley. He had retained Dion O'Banion's old flower shop as his office, and in the company of Paddy Murray, Sam Peller, WW O'Brien and Benny Jacobs, was returning there when caught in an ambush and killed by machine gun fire.

Murray was also killed; and O'Brien, Jacobs and Peller were seriously wounded. Of course, the surviving victims would not identify their assailants, and of course Capone made statements to the press expounding his liking for Weiss, and how sad it was that he had died. The only underworld figures of any notoriety to attend Weiss' funeral were 'Schemer' Drucci and 'Bugs' Moran, now the leaders of the gang.

Previous to this turn of events, the Joe Saltis-Frank McErlane Gang had been in leaning in Weiss' direction, and had infringed on Capone territory. After Weiss' murder, the Saltis/McErlane Gang became eager for peace with Capone. Through channels, they contacted underworld 'gray eminence' Maxie Eisen, who offered to contact Capone about a general armistice.

After two preparatory meetings in the office of Billy Skidmore, a notorious 'fixer,' it was agreed that a meeting of all Chicago gang leaders and their chief lieutenants would take place at the Hotel Sherman, near city hall and police headquarters. Capone, Drucci, Moran, the West Side O'Donnell brothers, Ralph Sheldon and Maxie Eisen (for the Saltis-McErlane Gang) were present, as were other important factors of each gang.

The meeting essentially re-established the 'peaceful cooperation' policy that Torrio had set forth years before, but this time, the result was that Capone walked out of the meeting as the undisputed king of the Chicago underworld, with a huge chunk of Chicago—and most of the suburbs—under his direct control. After the meeting, the gangsters repaired to Esposito's Bella Napoli Cafe for 'a feast of ghouls,' as a reporter on the scene described it. As they got drunker and drunker, the mobsters waxed ever more teasing, ever more maudlin about the times they'd tried to bump each other off—now of course, that the inter-gang conflicts were 'all over.'

Peace of sorts settled on gangland, as each mob settled down to its extortion, bootlegging, mugging, white slave kidnappings and working general mayhem upon the populace. Another judicial travesty was about to occur with the granting of re-trial for Scalise and Anselmi, on the grounds that if they were guilty of murder, their sentence was 'but a mockery of justice,' and if they were guilty only of manslaughter, then the defendants were being done 'an injustice' with such a harsh sentence.

The two were released from Joliet on $25,000 bail to await the retrial. Meanwhile, 'Big Bill' Thompson was readying, in late 1926, for the 1927 mayoral election year. Though he'd been practically thrown out of office in his 1923 bid for re-election, losing by a landslide to Judge Dever, Thompson was a showman who would stop at nothing to 'feed at the trough again.'

Way back in 1923–24, he had organized a highly publicized and totally meretricious expedition to study the habits of the strange amphibious walking fish of the South Seas. 'Big Bill' was provided with a boat and personnel with which to make the journey. The boat had a figurehead that was none other than Big Bill himself, and was fully equipped to transport Thompson and his beery colleagues to far ports in search of their quarry.

With cheering thousands lining the shores, the eponymous *Big Bill* sailed down the Chicago River into Lake Michigan, and thence toward New Orleans. Thompson himself went ashore before they made it to Louisiana, and hurried back to Illinois to consolidate his publicity gains, working to help re-elect Governor Small, and patching things up with disaffected crony, State's Attorney General Crowe. Thompson was preparing for the next election.

His platform for the 1926–27 mayoral campaign contained such utterly ridiculous points as education reform to remove a non-existent 'British slant' from Chicago public School textbooks, and the statement, concerning Prohibition, 'I'm wetter than the middle of the Atlantic Ocean.' Thompson baldly promised to make Chicago a wide open town.

Meanwhile, the treaty that had been forged between Chicago's gangs was already falling apart. Hilary Clements, a beer runner from the Ralph Sheldon Gang, was making encroachments upon Saltis-McErlane territory. Instead of submitting this infraction to 'council arbitration,' Saltis had Clements killed on 30 December 1926, just in time to seal the old year with blood. Sheldon complained to Capone, who agreed that disciplinary action was called for.

However, Capone was shortly to have similar 'business' of his own to take care of. It all began when Moran and Drucci, kicking under the constraints of the treaty, and full of hatred for Capone, decided to 'hit him in a very personal place.'

Theodore 'The Greek' Anton idolized Capone, and was in fact one of Capone's closest friends. He loved to recite tales of 'Snorky's' generosity, leaving out the means by which he could afford to be so generous. Anton had a popular restaurant located above the Hawthorne Smoke Shop. On the night of 6 January 1927, Capone was having a late snack, sitting

Ralph Sheldon's worries were more than the Saltis Gang (see text). His gang also fought the Charlie Birger Gang *(below)* in a liquor war in 1926. Birger afterward went into hiding.

and chatting with Anton in a booth of his restaurant. Anton went to greet some customers at the door.

The 'customers' turned out to be Moran and company, who pushed Anton into their car and took him for the proverbial 'ride.' His mutilated body was found in a quick-lime pit the next day. Capone took a jaunt to the gangster haven of Hot Springs, Arkansas, with Schemer Drucci on his trail. Drucci tried to kill him with a shotgun, but missed. Capone resolved to eliminate the Moran-Drucci Gang in the most pungent way possible.

Capone's life was getting very complicated. He also had to take care of Ralph Sheldon's complaint against Joe Saltis, and therefore Saltis-McErlane henchmen Lefty Koncil and Charlie Hubacek were executed on 11 March 1927.

Meanwhile, there was an election rig. As 5 April 1927 drew near, Capone's Hotel Metropole suite became an annex to the Thompson campaign headquarters in the Hotel Sherman. Messengers scurried to and fro between the hotels with messages and money. Capone manned the nine telephones on his big mahogany desk, giving orders to killers, bombers, kidnappers and muggers throughout the city, preparing the way for a 'peaceful' election day.

Moran and Drucci were heavy Thompson fans, too, and Drucci, leading a band of thugs bent on intimidating 42nd Ward Alderman Dorsey Crowe, broke into Crowe's office the day before the election, made a mess of the office and beat up Crowe's secretary. Later that same day, Drucci was picked up for questioning. On the way to the station, he threatened the officers and tried to grab Detective Dan Healy's gun. Healy shot Drucci four times.

When Drucci's lawyer wanted to press a charge for murder against Healy, Chief of Detectives William Schoemaker said 'I don't know anything about any murder. I know Drucci was killed trying to take a gun away from an officer. We're having a *medal* struck for Healy.' Drucci was buried in unconsecrated ground. With Drucci dead, the gang was now under the leadership of George 'Bugs' Moran.

Come election day, Mayor Dever had the polling places surrounded with police, and installed roving teams of heavily-armed detectives in every precinct. The fix already having been accomplished by weeks of intimidation and bribes, what remained to be done was accomplished when numerous Dever supporters were prevented from voting by thugs with guns who met voters on their way to the polls.

Thompson won by 83,072 votes, and promptly installed in every appointee position every boodler he owed a favor to, including Daniel Serritella as City Sealer (department of weights and measures) who conspired with crooked mer-

chants to give Chicago consumers less than they thought they were getting: Serritella was also Capone's agent in the City Council. Thompson rearranged city departments in such a way that it was now possible to buy City Hall and the police department, lock, stock and barrel.

Within a month after the election, Capone enlarged his Hotel Metropole headquarters to 50 rooms, using the Hawthorne Inn as a secondary headquarters. Hotel Metropole was centrally located, with easy access to both of these institutions: a steady stream of 'cooperative public servants' circulated to and from work by way of the hotel.

In June of that year, Scalise and Anselmi were acquitted in yet another ridiculous trial, typified by the fact that nearly 100 prospective jurors were excused by reason of their extreme fear.

There then followed the 'War of Sicilian Succession,' in which Joseph Aiello—jealous over Tony Lombardo's accession to the presidency of the Unione Siciliane—set in motion an intensely bloody sequence of events that was to climax in the St Valentine's Day Massacre.

The Aiellos—Joe, Dominick, Tony and Andrew (plus five other brothers who figured less prominently in the family 'business')—had originally been suppliers of sugar for the Genna's rotgut booze business. After the Gennas had been eliminated from gangland contention, the Aiellos determined to take over the rotgut business themselves. Lombardo's rule as President of the Unione cut into their operations in Little Italy.

They set to work undermining Merlo's position by sending agitators to spread rumors at other Unione chapters across the country. The result was that numerous of their 'agents' were swiftly murdered by friends of Merlo and Capone. Still, the Aiellos tried again and again to prevail. Soon enough, they formed a coalition with Bugs Moran, Billy Skidmore the fixer, Barney Bertche and Jack Zuta, the latter two being itinerate gunmen.

The clique spread the word that a $50,000 bounty was fixed on Al 'Snorky' Capone's head. Swiftly, the out-of-town gunmen arrived, and swiftly they died: between May and October, New York gunman Tony Torchio, Cleveland gunman Samuel Valente and St Louis gunmen Anthony Russo and Vincent Spicuzza were found dead, each with his undrawn gun in a back alley, and each with 'Machine Gun' Jack McGurn's trademark nickel pressed into his hand.

Below left: Charlie Birger (see caption, page 29) meets his end. *Below:* 'Big Bill' Thompson (with kazoo) on election night, 5 April 1927. Note the suspiciously premature headline.

Then the Aiellos offered the chef at the Little Italy Cafe — one of Capone's favorite eateries — $10,000 to lace Capone's soup with prussic acid. The chef told Capone, and he now knew exactly who was gunning for him. Capone's killers claimed six Aiello hirelings within a month, as follows: Lawrence La Presta on 1 June, Diego Attlomionte on 29 June, Numio Jamericco and Lorenzo Alagno on 30 June, Giovanni Blaudins on 11 July and Dominic Cinderella on 17 July. McGurn and fellow killer Orchell DeGrazio were suspected in at least one of the killings, but no indictment was returned.

The Chicago Police Department made a great amount of noise, and swore it would clean the city entirely of mobsters. Chief Detective William O'Connor set up a volunteer force of 500 machine gun and armored car-equipped detectives who were to 'shoot to kill' when they saw any mobsters. On 22 November, they raided the offices of The Chicago Candy Jobber's Union and arrested 45 mobsters for intimidation and violence against candy industry workers.

Frank Herbert, Joe Saltis' body guard, was killed as he attempted an escape. That same day, acting on a tip, they searched an apartment in a building at 4442 Washington Boulevard that overlooked Tony Lombardo's front door. Here, the police found several machine guns, apparently ready to be taken up by gunners at a moment's notice. Then,

acting further on the same tip, they raided a house at 7002 North Western Avenue, where they located a large cache of dynamite, and a key to a room in the Rex Hotel, on Ashland Avenue.

They raided the hotel room, bursting in upon Joe Aiello, two of his cousins and a hired gun from Milwaukee, Angelo Lo Mantio. Lo Mantio readily confessed that Aiello had hired him to kill Capone and Lombardo, and he led them to a sniper's nest that overlooked the entrance of Alderman Michael 'Hinky Dink' Kenna's cigar store, where Capone often visited for the latest news from 'the Dink's' ward.

An hour after Aiello and Lo Mantio were brought in, six taxis pulled up outside of the police station, and 25 men emerged from them. A detective noticed this, and at first thought that they were officials of some sort coming to pay a visit. When he saw all but three of them duck into alleys and doorways, he became suspicious. When the trio that was in the open began walking toward the door, it became obvious that they were armed. The police recognized the leader as Louis Campagna, a Capone import from New York, and they realized that the Capone mob intended to lay siege to the police station, hoping to kill Aiello.

A mob of policemen grabbed and disarmed Campagna and his two companions, hustling them into the cell next to Aiello. In another cell nearby, they posted an undercover

man of Sicilian extraction, who listened and interpreted as the gangsters spoke in Italian. Campagna said 'You're dead, friend, you're dead. You won't get to the end of the street still walking.'

Aiello pled with him, saying 'Give me 14 days and I'll sell my stores, house and everything, and quit Chicago for good. Can't we settle this? Think of my wife and baby.' When he was released from custody, the police escorted him to a taxi, and he made it home unscathed.

Capone, by this time, was feeling that, with Aiello (at least temporarily) subdued, there would be no hindrance to his domination of Chicago. He hadn't counted on Mayor 'Big Bill' Thompson's political aspirations. The 1928 presidential primary was but a year away, and Calvin Coolidge announced that he was not going to run for re-election as President of the US. America was still wallowing in the 'free and easy money' of the 'Roaring Twenties.' This tempted Thompson's gargantuan appetite—why not sit at the biggest 'trough' of all? He realized that Capone's unfettered presence could potentially be an embarrassment to any such aspiration—totally forgetting, of course, his own terrible reputation.

Thompson ordered the police to clamp down on Capone's operations. Capone, insulted that an administration into which he had poured so much graft money should turn on him so, made a well-publicized visit to Los Angeles, telling 'the good citizens of Chicago to get their own booze.' After a day's stay in the Los Angeles Biltmore, he was told by the Los Angeles chief of police to get out of town. He returned to Chicago, determined to obtain a place of refuge in America's now obviously unpredictable political climate. This led him to buy a summer home in Miami, on Palm Island in Biscayne Bay.

Thompson, meanwhile, realized that he, as the unmitigated buffoon of American politics, had no chance of ever becoming president, and he returned Chicago to a laissez-faire relationship to crime. There were political cronies to boost—especially State's Attorney Crowe and Governor Small, and the various pork barrel and pro-mob politicians in Chicago.

Thompson patched up his relationship with Capone, and set the stage for a primary that was renowned for its violence. It was dubbed 'the Pineapple Primary,' an appellation deriving from the military slang for 'hand grenade.' This primary was a battle for Republican nominees to state and county offices. On one side stood Senator Charles S

Below left: The Los Angeles Biltmore, the only hotel that ever threw Al Capone out (see text, this page). *Below:* Capone's winter estate (and refuge) on Palm Island, in Biscayne Bay, Florida.

Deneen's conservative slate; on the other stood 'Big Bill' Thompson's wide-open cronies.

On 27 January 1928, the homes of Thompson-appointed City Controller Charles Fitzmorris and Commissioner of Public Service William Reed were bombed, and on 11 February, Secretary to the State's Attorney Lawrence Cuneo's home was bombed. The Thompsonites knew that this was the work of pro-Deneen mobster Joseph 'Diamond Joe' Esposito. On 21 March, Esposito was told by phone, and in person, to 'get out of town or get killed.'

That evening, out for a stroll with his bodyguards, Esposito was slain in a drive-by shooting. Ironically, his bodyguards dropped to the pavement in time, but Esposito caught the full fury of the pistol and shotgun attack. The day after the funeral, Senator Deneen's house was wrecked by a

At left, below and below right: **Various police and FBI agents confiscate booze, and smash a still. Capone's alcohol profits bought graft protection for his rackets, but when President Calvin Coolidge** *(below left)* **refused re-election, 'Big Bill' Thompson's ambition was more compelling than the graft (see text, page 33).**

bomb, and his friend, Judge John Swanson, narrowly missed being eradicated by a grenade thrown from a passing car.

Thompson and State's Attorney Robert Crowe tried to pin all the blame on Deneen and his faction, and in reaction to this hypocrisy, the Chicago Crime Commission shifted its support from Crowe and Thompson to Deneen. President Coolidge was urged to send the US Marines to Chicago, but he declined to do so. On Easter Sunday, the clergy of Chicago spoke out against the Small-Thompson-Crowe faction: 'We have a governor who ought to be in the penitentiary… Ours is a government of bombs and bums…Oh Lord! May there be an awakening of public spirit and consciousness….'

On the day of the primary, 10 April, party hacks stuffed ballot boxes and rigged the voting lists with names of deceased, derelict and totally fictitious people. Capone directed his mobsters—heavily outnumbering the Deneen forces—in a program of intimidation whereby they dragged scrupulous election officials away from their posts, kidnapped others and generally were allowed by corrupt police to enact all forms of electoral illegality in the name of getting the Thompson slate installed.   Murder was also a

feature of the day: Octavius Granady, a black attorney, was the only one who had dared challenge 'Boss' Eller's primacy in the 12th Ward. Granady was slain by shots fired from a car full of hoods.

All the bombs and violence had caused an unforseen effect: the voter turnout was more than twice that predicted; the Thompsonites, even with their violence and intimidation, were defeated by a landslide of votes that were far more in reaction against Thompson and his cronies Governor Small and State's Attorney Crow than actually for the Deneen axis.

Thompson, still mayor but with his wide base of support torn away from him, was abashed but not repentant. Despite the pre-primary crackdown on Capone, and the subsequent preparations for the primary, gangland killings continued, and especially the 'War of Sicilian Succession' had continued without abatement. The Unione Siciliane had been renamed with the Americanized monicker of 'The Italo-American Union.' Also, Joe Aiello continued to militate for his claim to the Union's Chicago presidency, despite Capone.

Italo-American Union National President Frank Yale was

deemed to be double-crossing Capone by encouraging, from his base in New York, the Aiello claim to the Chicago presidency, and was also aiding shipment hijackings of Capone liquor in Ohio.

Frank Yale was gunned down on 1 July 1927, by Capone mobsters who had detoured via New York, on their way back to Chicago from the new Capone outpost in Florida. The weapons—revolvers and a Thompson submachine gun—were all traced back to Capone. A grand jury inquest was held, and New York Police Commissioner Grover Whalen stated, 'In my opinion, there was enough evidence not only to get an indictment, but a conviction as well.' Due to gangland machinations, an indictment was never returned.

It can be seen from the following series of events that the Presidency of the Chicago Chapter of the Italo-American Union was a 'perilous seat,' indeed.

On 7 September 1927, Chicago Chapter President Tony Lombardo was strolling home from the organization's head-quarters. After he and his bodyguards—Joseph Ferraro and Joseph Lolordo—had advanced half a block on Madison Street, they were caught in an ambush by two Aiello thugs who shot them in the back. Only Lolordo survived, and was to see his older brother Pasquale Lolordo succeed to the Presidency of the Italo-American Union on 14 September.

Lolordo's opponent in the election, Peter Rizzito, was gunned down for no apparent reason shortly afterward. Pasquale Lolordo himself was killed by Joe Aiello and two henchmen in his own home while trying to make an alliance with them in the spring of 1928.

After Lolordo's death, Capone mobster Joseph 'Hop Toad' Giunta became the President of the Italo-American Union. He lasted until his 'traitor's death' at Capone's hands in May of 1929. Then Joe Aiello had his day as President: he lasted a little over a year.

On the evening of 23 October 1930, Aiello was machine gunned to death in front of a close friend's house by Alphonse 'Al' Mineo, a killer from 'Joe the Boss' Masseria's gang in New York. It turns out that Lucky Luciano had decided to help Capone with his Aiello feud (and help himself out at the same time), by convincing 'Joe the Boss' that Aiello had engineered a killing against Masseria lieutenant Pietro 'The Clutching Hand' Morello. This is discussed more fully in the Lucky Luciano segment of this text.

Capone had meanwhile moved his operations center from the Hotel Metropole to the third and fourth floors of the once-elite Hotel Lexington. The management installed a gourmet kitchen on the fourth floor of the 10-floor structure exclusively for Capone's entourage, and the chef tasted every one of Capone's meals in advance, to assure that the food, and the drink, had not been poisoned.

In the midst of the above-related 'War of Sicilian Succession,' Chicago still had to prepare for the 1928 national election. In light of the violent 'Pineapple Primary,' Frank Loesch, President of the Chicago Crime Commission, asked for an audience to plead with Capone for peace in the upcoming election. Loesch realized that all the official agencies under Thompson were hopelessly corrupt, and would be—at least until the elections. It made sense to approach Capone, therefore, in hopes that his army of thugs and corrupted policemen might be turned toward keeping the peace for a change.

This appealed to 'Snorky's' vanity—even if the election

were to result in reform, he had proven his ability to survive, and this request was a testament to the kind of 'clout' that he then enjoyed in Chicago. Loesch, taken aback by Capone's arrogant demeanor, burst out: 'Now look here, Capone—will you help me by keeping your damned cutthroats and hoodlums from interfering with the polling booths?'

Capone replied 'Sure, I'll give them the word because they're all dagos...but what about this Saltis gang of micks on the West Side? Do you want me to give them the works, too?'

Loesch answered in the affirmative. Capone's next answer confirmed what the public had only known as general knowledge about the connection of thugs and crooked authority: 'All right, I'll have the cops send over squad cars the night before the election and jug all of the hoodlums and keep 'em in the cooler until the polls close.'

It went just as Capone had said, and it was a peaceful, unrigged election that resulted in a Republican victory that was, on the local level, a repudiation of 'Big Bill' Thompson by his own party. In the national elections, Herbert Hoover beat Al Smith. While Smith had been a relatively 'tolerant' candidate, Hoover was absolutely determined to end the reign of Al Capone, by now the most notorious mobster in America.

The mob that had descended from the Dion O'Banion Gang, and was now being led by Bugs Moran was still active. Its surviving personnel included such central gang members as Willie Marks, second in command and Moran's body-guard; Frank and Pete Gusenberg, specialists in burglary and train robbery; John May, a safecracker; Ted Newberry, head whiskey salesman; Al Weinshank, director of speakeasies, and a leading labor racketeer; Jim 'Clark' Kashelleck, Moran's brother-in-law and head gunman; and industrial racketeer Adam Heyer, owner of the SMC Cartage Company, a garage at 2122 North Clark Street where Moran's mob kept its booze, trucks and cars.

Capone had an agreement with Detroit's Purple Gang that supplied him with rivers of outlaw whiskey called Old Log Cabin. Moran was in turn supplied with Old Log Cabin by Capone. Hating Capone eventually superseded Moran's gangland business sense, and he terminated the Old Log Cabin arrangement by saying that the whiskey was good, but the price was too high.

Moran obtained a Canadian whiskey supply, and this cheaper product was inferior to Old Log Cabin, and pocketing the difference, he charged his customers the same price as he had for Capone's whiskey. Sales of the new product were very poor, and Moran pled with Capone to restore him to the Old Log Cabin rolls. Capone had already found another customer, and therefore, Moran was out of luck.

Moran decided to hijack his share of Old Log Cabin. When consignment after consignment was hijacked en route from Detroit to Chicago, Capone and the Purple Gang grew suspicious of Moran, and laid a trap for him by slipping a spy into the midst of his gang. This 'secret agent' let on to Moran that he knew when Purple Gang shipments were taking place: representing himself as an expert hijacker, he delivered a number of cargoes to Moran and his thugs, setting them up for the most notorious of gangland massacres.

Capone consolidated his plan, and had the spy call Moran on the evening of 13 February 1929. He made arrangements

At right: **Just after the St Valentine's Day Massacre (see text, these pages)—Capone's infamous revenge of 14 February 1929.**

to meet Moran the next day, at Heyer's North Clark Street garage at 10:30 in the morning. It was no accident that Capone chose to send 'his tender regards' to Bugs Moran on St Valentine's Day.

At 10:50 on the bitter cold morning of 14 February, several neighborhood residents noticed a black Packard sedan, of the kind used by detective squads, as it pulled up to the curb two doors north of the SMC Cartage Company Garage. Two men in police uniforms and three in civilian clothes emerged from the car and entered the garage.

Moments later, a sound like that of a jack hammer was heard issuing from inside the garage, and was followed by two muffled explosions. At 10:58, the civilians were seen marching back toward the Packard, their hands in the air, with the policemen behind them, guns drawn. They all got into the car and drove off.

Moran had been late for the supposed 'shipment' that morning, and as he and henchmen Willie Marks and Ted Newberry approached the garage, they saw the Packard pull up and disgorge its passengers. Moran and company faded into the shadows until 'the heat' was off.

After the Packard left, the landlady of a nearby apartment house, Mrs Jeanette Landesman, grew curious about the goings-on in the garage, and went to see for herself what had happened. The door was jammed shut. She asked one of her tenants force the door open with his shoulder, and he went inside, only to come running back with the news that the garage was 'full of dead men.' Thus the notorious 'St Valentine's Day Massacre' had occurred, and caused a trumpeting about reform in the popular press that actually did ring in new era, in which gangsters would no longer be quite as bold in American cities.

On the floor of the garage lay Moran mobsters Frank and Pete Gusenberg, John May, Al Weinshank, James Clark and Adam Heyer. Also slain was Dr Rheinhart H Schwimmer, a hanger-on who had inadvertently become proof that it is dangerous to play with mobsters. The men had been methodically sprayed back and forth with machine gun bullets, and Clark and May, apparently 'still kicking' after this treatment, then received shotgun wounds to the head.

The killers apparently hadn't noticed the flickering spark of life in Frank Gusenberg, who lived for two and one-half hours after the massacre, but refused to say who his assailants were. It has been theorized that Fred Burke and James Ray of the St Louis-based Egan's Rats Gang had been brought into town to masquerade as the 'policemen,' and Joseph Lolordo (younger brother of the murdered Italo-American Union president Pasquale Lolordo) and the two murderous buddies John Scalise and Albert Anselmi had portrayed the 'civilians.'

It was further supposed that the killers put the out-of-towners in front and feigned an arrest of the Moran Gang. Once they had them spread-eagled against the wall, the rest was all too easy. Then the masquerade continued, with the feigned 'arrest' of the 'civilians' being a cover for any suspicions that might have been aroused until the disguised killers got away.

Despite such speculation, no one was actually convicted for taking part in the St Valentine's Day Massacre. Capone was in Florida at the time, and had arranged to be talking with the Miami District Attorney at the very moment the killing was taking place. Assistant State's Attorney David Stansbury felt that he had established, within reason, that 'Machine Gun' Jack McGurn had made the payment arrangements, and that Joseph 'Hop Toad' Giunta (an Italo-American Union politico, whose monicker came from his love of dancing) was also implicated.

It was further evidenced that Capone's gang had set up lookout nests by the site of the massacre, to telephone the killers the moment Moran stepped into the garage. Moran was probably saved by his similarity and closeness in style of dress to the now-deceased Weinshank. The mobsters had mistaken the one for the other, and ordered the 'hit' too soon to include Moran among their victims.

Arrests were made, with little result. Jack McGurn's lawyers took advantage of the Illinois statute requiring the *nolle prossing* of a case if a defendant requests a trial in four terms of court and does not get one. Simple as it seems, McGurn's lawyers requested a trial on 28 May, 8 July, 15 August and 23 September, with the State mysteriously requesting an adjournment each time. On 2 December, the State was still not ready, and McGurn was a free man.

Fred Burke was finally tied to the killings through the then-new science of ballistic analysis. Arrested in Michigan the following year for the killing of a police officer, he was never to stand trial for the massacre, but died in Michigan State Penitentiary, in the course of a life sentence.

Adding a touch more confusion to an already frustrating case for criminologists, Alvin Karpis—a thief and murderer with the Ma Barker Gang—got to know many of the famous criminals of his day during his many years in prison. He claimed to have been told, years after it happened, that the St Valentine's Day Massacre had actually been done by a 'utility squad' of killers that had perpetrated killings for hire throughout the US.

These thugs were, ostensibly, Fred Burke, Claude Maddox, George Ziegler, Gus Winkler and 'Crane Neck' Nugent, with Ziegler doing double duty as the planner of the execution. Of course, Karpis had befriended Capone in prison, and might have bent the truth a bit, to clear his buddy.

It was not the end of murder, though—as long as there are gangs, there will be killings. Capone had started hearing disturbing things about Giunta, Scalise and Anselmi. Frank Rio had told him of Giunta's statement, 'I'm the big shot now,' in obvious reference to his presidency of the Italo-American Union, and in obvious disdain of Capone—who had put him in the presidency. Scalise and Anselmi had been installed by Giunta as his chief executive officers in the Union, and were feeling quite capable of shuffling off the trappings of loyal Capone men.

Capone felt that a test of Giunta's loyalty was in order. Early in May, 1929, he invited him, with Scalise and Anselmi, to dinner with Frank Rio and himself at the Hawthorne Inn.

During the dinner, he and Rio faked a quarrel in which Rio slapped Capone and stalked out.

The next day Giunta and company contacted Rio with an offer to combine forces against Capone. The four plotted and planned for several days, and then Rio reported back to Capone, who, feigning delight at their great success in the Union, invited the conspirators to a banquet in their honor. It was an honor they couldn't refuse, and they felt that they were really 'putting it to' Capone by accepting his hospitality while plotting to kill him.

It is an old mob custom to give an enemy a 'send-off feast,' if possible, before killing him. Long after midnight, the sated guests were smoking their after-dinner cigars. It had been a sumptuous dinner, and had Scalise, Anselmi and Giunta been alert, they might have detected that they were being set up, in an atmosphere of mellow conviviality. Suddenly, the joking and laughter stopped, and a dead calm settled over the crowded room. Most of the top men in the Capone mob were there, and all eyes turned to 'The Big Fellow.'

He leaned toward the guests of honor and slowly enunciated: 'So you thought I didn't know?' The three men were pinioned by fellow thugs, and were then bound to their chairs with wire. Capone took up a baseball bat he had placed behind a curtain, and thoroughly bludgeoned the thorax of each conspirator with it. Finally, an 'executioner' shot them each in the head. Their bodies were then taken out and dumped—a testament to Capone's hatred of disloyalty in his underlings. Needless to say, the three victims were thus rendered unfit for trial in the St Valentine's Day Massacre.

A week later, Capone's presence was requested at Lucky Luciano's conference in Atlantic City, which is further discussed in the segment of this book that deals with Lucky Luciano. Luciano's plan, backed and inspired by Torrio, was to reorganize the many gang factions in the US into large, autonomous regional bodies that would answer to a national 'board,' or council, composed of the most respected, and most powerful gang leaders.

The main secondary topic was the spate of adverse publicity that gang violence—especially as witnessed in Chicago. Luciano and Torrio, especially, wanted an end to it, as it had turned a public opinion heatedly against the gangs.

The immediate answer was public atonement, possible only by the sacrificing of a top mobster. Since Capone was the very hub of the most spectacular violence, and the public knew it, he was then asked by his fellow mobsters to take a 'dive' for a phony weapons arrest, and to spend the required time in a prearranged, friendly jail. That would appease the public.

And so Al 'Snorky' Capone had himself arrested by corrupted policemen in Irving 'Waxey Gordon' Wexler's territory, Philadelphia. The Capone family, especially Capone's mother and sister Mafalda, felt simply that Al was an important businessman, and with all the recent violence, he was only trying to protect himself by carrying a concealed pistol. The papers, just as the gang had hoped, made much of the arrest, and it seemed that justice was being done.

Sentenced to a year in prison, Capone was able to conduct 'business' while in jail, especially after his transfer to Eastern

At right: **Al and Ralph (foreground) Capone in Florida. Ralph's nickname was 'Bottles.' His job was to intimidate prospective buyers into buying Capone liquor.**

Penitentiary, where he was allowed to install a rug, a lamp and bookshelves in his cell. He had begun his sentence in June, 1929, and knocked two months off his time by being a model prisoner. In fact, Dr Herbert M Goddard—who performed an emergency tonsillectomy on Capone at Eastern—exclaimed, 'He would have made good anywhere….' In itself, this was a tragic comment, considering where and how Al Capone *had* made good.

On 16 March 1930, Capone left the prison under cover, in the warden's car, and was transported to the town of Graterford, where he was detained to serve the one day remaining in his sentence before being released. This procedure was adopted to foil reporters, publicity seekers and assassins who would probably await Capone's release, and create turmoil at the prison gates. The next day, as a mock release was being staged, Capone was speeding on his way back to Chicago in the company of trusted gang members.

When he arrived in Chicago, the media sought him everywhere, even trying to bribe his son for news of Al's whereabouts. It was all to no avail. Capone spent a few days in hiding, and a few days at the Hawthorne Inn, reviewing the gang's sorry financial situation.

Captain John Stege of the Chicago Police Department had called for Capone to be run out of town as soon as he surfaced. When Capone did surface, he did so with his lawyer Thomas Nash. Stege ordered Capone out of town, and Nash said he couldn't do so without an arrest warrant, adding erroneously that 'Lenin and Trotsky rebelled at that kind of treatment.' Ironically like Capone, Lenin and Trotsky murdered anyone who stood in their way.

Stege replied, 'I hope Capone goes to Russia.'

In fact, while Capone had been in jail, America had become the sort of 'Russia' that Stege had in mind: two major events had occurred that would greatly affect the Capone Gang. The first was the advent of the Great Depression, which severely limited Capone's vice and booze customers' spending money, and thus dramatically decreased Capone Gang revenues.

The other was more directly focused on Capone himself. The average citizens of Chicago had long complained of the gangsterism in their city, and their chief public voice was Colonel Frank Knox of the Chicago *Daily News*. Heeding Knox' newspaper editorials and repeated supplications by mail, phone and in person, the US Justice Department engineered a two-pronged attack against Capone and his gang.

The 'first prong' was Federal Agent Eliot Ness and his Special Investigation Squad—a 'flying squad' of government prohibition agents—were to persistently raid Capone's breweries and distilleries, and thus would hamper Capone financially.

The 'second prong' was the Internal Revenue Service who had already begun to garner evidence on Capone's blatant non-payment of income tax. The aim of the IRS was to send Capone himself to prison for more than a few years.

The idea for Ness's Special Investigation Squad was created during meetings of the Chicago Crime Commission and 'The Secret Six.' This latter was so named because the six private citizens who composed the group were a 'think tank' dedicated to legally eliminating corruption in Chicago, and were thus ever under threat of mob reprisals: they considered anonymity essential to their effectiveness.

Eliot Ness, leader of the Special Investigation Squad, was an unusually upright and courageous man of 26 years. To go up against Capone was to face almost certain death. Ness's activities were indeed a shock to Chicago's gangsters in that, for the first time, agents of the Prohibition Department were doing their job: prohibition agents had theretofore been the most corruptible of the corrupt, as bribes were plentiful.

He was sharp and intelligent—having a doctorate degree from the University of Chicago—and hated mob activity, as he clearly saw the plight of its multitudinous victims. He proved to be invulnerable to bribes, and he was strongly motivated by something more than career ambition—which was, after all, another major avenue of corruption for many 'public servants.' Ness was concerned that the world of future generations was being tainted, and made infinitely more difficult, by the actions of such men as Capone.

To strike at Capone's financial base was also to strike at his ability to bribe, and therefore resulted in increased vulnerability for the gang's operations. For the task, Ness had hand-picked, from thousands of government personnel files, a team of trustworthy agents: Marty Lahart, Sam Seager, Barney Cloonan, Lyle Chapman, Tom Friel, Joe Leeson, Mike King, Paul Robsky, Bill Gardner and Frank Basile.

Their dramatic raids on Capone breweries and distilleries cost Capone millions of dollars in equipment, alcohol and trucks. The Ness raids also resulted in the regular jailing of known Capone associates, and thus the light of judicial scrutiny was focused more intensely on the Capone Gang's bootlegging operations.

Internal Revenue Service Enforcement Branch Chief Elmer Irey decided to make several 'test runs' with the income tax attack, before trying it on the central target: Al 'Scarface' Capone. The IRS was armed with a powerful weapon: the taxability of illegal income. It had recently been confirmed in federal court—in a successful case against bootlegger Manley Sullivan—that a taxpayer was liable for income tax assessment, no matter the legality of his income.

Irey chose Tax Investigations Agent Frank J Wilson to head the team that was to work on the cases. Wilson was an extremely sober individual, and was said to 'sweat ice water.' The first mobsters targeted were Terry Druggan and Frank Lake, the eccentric dress-alike bootleggers who masked their operations with a front called 'The Standard Beverage Corporation.'

Druggan and Lake had already been assessed taxes, for the years 1922–24, totalling $615,917—yet they disregarded IRS demands for payment until the tax court ruling. Then they offered a settlement of $50,000, together with a tally sheet of their assets. The government refused the offer and set Wilson to work on the case: he uncovered millions of dollars in undeclared assets, and the two pled guilty.

Legal maneuvering stalled their prison dates until 1932, when Druggan commenced his sentence of two and one-half years, and Lake commenced his sentence of 18 months, in Leavenworth Federal Penitentiary.

The next test case was Al's less-cautious brother Ralph Capone. Working in Chicago was a young IRS agent named Eddie Waters, a zealous fellow who continually needled the gangsters about paying their income taxes. After three years of this treatment, Ralph Capone agreed to pay up if Waters would do his returns for him. Ralph supplied figures for the

At right: **Eliot Ness, post-Chicago. Ness was 26 years old when he began shutting down the Capone breweries—cutting Capone's income for graft. Ness' indictment helped to send 'Al' to prison.**

years 1922–25 that translated into a modest tax liability of $4065. Ralph signed the form, but never bothered to pay the tax.

The next year, the IRS moved to seize his property. Ralph hurried to the tax collector's office, and pled poverty, offering $1000 as a compromise payment. Tax chief Irey was aghast at such an obvious lie. He set a tenacious investigator, Nels E Tessem, to work on the Ralph Capone case. Ralph Capone realized he was then under investigation, and hurriedly upped his offer to $2500, but it was too late.

During this same time, federal agents raided a Cicero gambling house, and the 'owner,' Oliver Ellis, admitted under threat of income tax audit that a man he had never seen—'James Carroll'—and not he, actually owned the gambling house. Following the name Carroll to an account in the Pinkert State Bank, tenacious Nels Tessem traced the money in that account back through a series of transfers that had been made from others accounts.These accounts were listed under five aliases, all of them leading back to an original depositor: Ralph Capone.

Having uncovered Ralph's hidden assets, Tessem then tracked down merchants to whom checks from the various accounts had been paid. Enough of them could substantiate that Ralph Capone was indeed the man who wrote those checks, that a grand jury returned seven indictments against him.

Arrested on 8 October 1929, Ralph Capone was tried. In April, 1930, he was sentenced to a $10,000 fine and three years in prison. The Pinkert State Bank records also led to the prosecutors to trace a certain 'JV Dunbar,' to whom $250,000 in cashier's checks had been issued. 'Dunbar,' it turned out, was a Capone gambling house cashier named Fred Ries. From an informer, it was learned that Ries was hiding out in St Louis.

One of the biggest breaks in the IRS case was so unexpected that it had to be pure providence. Ries had a phobia of insects, and, having been placed in a grungy jail in Danville, Illinois, his fear of the cockroaches in the jail overwhelmed his fear of mob repercussions, and he 'sang like a canary.'

Ries' testimony enabled a grand jury to indict Capone business manager Jake Guzik on income tax fraud. The trial began on 3 October 1930, and with Ries on the witness stand, plus $144,000 in cashier's checks endorsed by Guzik, a conviction was achieved on 18 November.

It was obvious that a new era in gangster trials had dawned. Guzik received a sentence of $17,500 in fines and five years in federal prison. Next came an indictment of mob treasurer Frank Nitti, also fueled by Ries' testimony. On 20 December of that same year, Nitti pled guilty to evasion of $158,823 in income taxes. His sentence included fines of $10,000 and an 18-month prison term.

The government sought some way of protecting Ries from the dire fate that the mob would surely inflict on him for his 'singing.' A federal witness protection program did not yet exist, and any such protection had to be improvised. The Secret Six contributed $10,000, so that Ries could be transported to a dwelling in South America, with a round-the-clock guard donated by the federal government. Ries would live to testify in future legal action against the mob.

The case dossier against Capone himself had actually been started in 1928. Capone was extremely well protected, however, and it would take a lot of digging to weed him out.

Delving into Capone's Miami Beach Bank accounts in the fall of that year, an IRS agent detected an effort on the part of that bank to conceal information. This was confirmed by a message from another Miami area bank that the Miami Beach Bank had solicited (and failed to obtain) their services in attempting to launder certain checks that were made out to Capone.

This tip led to investigations of other possible 'laundering' banks on the outskirts of Miami. Soon, the IRS was able to determine the financial arrangements whereby Capone bought his Palm Island house. Working closely with Miami officials, the investigation of that part of Capone's holdings was proceeding steadily.

With the Nitti and Guzik convictions accomplished, IRS Inspector Wilson himself was ready to leap into the Capone investigation full force. Wilson chose his team for this especially difficult and very dangerous task: in addition to the stalwart Nels Tessem, there were William Hodgins, Clarence Converse, James N Sullivan and Michael Malone. Malone was an expert infiltrator, and had dark Mediterranean looks, which he used to masquerade as persons from a number of ethnic backgrounds.

The challenge was to clearly define and prove Capone's taxable income—which by definition, was any amount he made in any one year over $5000. Capone's most prized nickname was 'Snorky'—underworld slang for one having refined taste. Therefore, an exhaustive search was conducted of Miami- and Chicago-area shops, real estate agents, restaurants and any other kind of establishment with which Capone, as a consumer, might have dealt.

They uncovered expenditures including $7000 worth of paid invoices for suits; $1500 per week hotel bills; $40,000 for the Palm Island house; $39,000 worth of phone calls; $20,000 worth of silverware; $18,000 for two docks, a boathouse and a second garage; and miscellaneous other items, totalling purchases commensurate with $165,000 of taxable income.

Still, Wilson realized that this was only a small percentage of the enormous cash intake that Capone collected from his huge criminal empire. While it would not doubt serve to substantiate Capone's hidden income, circumstantial evidence such as these expenditures would not be enough to win a conviction. The IRS needed more solid evidence. Special Agent Sullivan was assigned to investigating the brothels.

Searching for a prostitute who would be likely to talk and tell the truth without fear of reprisals was his task: he haunted the courthouse on Saturday nights, sizing up each girl as she was brought in. He found his mark in a woman who was obviously at the end of her career: for $50 per week—far more than she was earning in the brothel—she became an IRS spy.

Malone, meanwhile, had checked into the Hotel Lexington, under the alias 'Michael Lepito.' When Capone mobsters inquired as to his business, he intimated that he was a fugitive, interested only in 'keeping quiet.' Befriended by the mob, he was allowed to join in several poker games. He, Sullivan and Wilson uncovered a lot of useful information, but again the essential link, descrying the linkage by which Capone received millions from the gambling houses, brothels and bootlegging, was not there.

Chicago violence meanwhile continued. In January of 1930, Frank McErlane was attacked by a killer usually employed by his partner Joe Saltis. The killer, 'Dingbat' O'Berta, and a second gunman were aiming to usurp McErlane's place in the gang. Wounded in the leg, McErlane was confined to a hospital, and there was attacked again by O'Berta and a crony. Again, McErlane survived the attack, and apparently decided to end the feud in the typical gangland style. On 5 March, Dingbat and his driver were hijacked and taken for 'a ride' in Dingbat's own car. Both men were riddled with bullets.

In April, Capone's lawyer contacted Wilson to say that Capone wanted to come in and 'straighten things out.' When they arrived at Wilson's office, Capone denied any interest in the mob empire, and his lawyer intimated that Al, festooned with diamonds as he sat there, was actually rather poor. Wilson continued questioning—about the racetracks, about the casinos, about the Hawthorne Smoke Shop. Capone got angry, saying:

'They're trying to push me around, but I'll take care of myself….How's your wife, Wilson? You be sure to take care of yourself.' Wilson, undaunted, later arranged an interview with Jake Lingle, an ace crime reporter for the Chicago *Tribune*. Lingle was rumored to know Capone far better than most people realized. The meeting was arranged for 10 June, but Lingle was killed the morning of 9 June.

For a time, it was speculated that, as Lingle had been 'in the know' with the mob, he had been silenced because he had 'hot information.' Another story was that many of the reporters in Chicago were on the 'take' like everyone else seemed to be, and Lingle had a good 'cover' as a trusted reporter for the *Tribune*.

The rumors that surrounded the case (originating from various questionable sources) indicated that Lingle was in the extortion racket. One story had it that Lingle's chief 'mark' was a Moran-backed speakeasy that Lingle 'protected,' with his reportage and connections, for 10 percent of the take. The speakeasy, the Sheridan Wave Club on Waveland Avenue, was closed for lack of business. A year lapsed before 'new owners,' Julian Kaufman and Joey Brooks, announced plans to re-open it. Lingle approached them and demanded 50 percent of the take or he'd call the police and have it closed up again.

The mobsters deemed that he should part with his life rather than they with their money, and so, Lingle was murdered on 9 June. On 30 June, Moran's business manager and whoremonger Jack Zuta was brought in for questioning. Zuta was the frailest of frail reeds, and was easily frightened. When the mob learned that Zuta was to be interrogated by the tenacious State's Attorney Chief Investigator Patrick Roche, they were concerned that Zuta would talk.

They worried so much that when Zuta was released, they sent a hit squad to kill him. Somehow, Zuta survived, and fled to Wisconsin, assuming an alias. At the scene of the attempted hit, a revolver with typical Capone Gang markings to disguise the serial number was found, and, upon ballistic analysis, turned out to be one that had been used by Sam 'Golf Bag' Hunt in an assault the month before.

Below: Sedans like this Cadillac were good for prestige (or drive-by shooting)—but with Frank Wilson, Eliot Ness and the federal government closing in, Capone, *et al*, were not in a buying mood.

Therefore, it was not just a Moran operation, and after five men blasted Zuta to pieces in his hideout on 1 August, ballistic analysis revealed that several of the 16 bullets extracted from his body belonged to yet another Hunt weapon. The questions raised by Lingle's death caused a great deal of inconvenience for Capone.

Investigator Roche was joined in his task by Charles Rathbun, and they set about with a 'flying squad' of detectives, who proceeded to dismantle every speakeasy, whorehouse and gambling den in Chicago and vicinity, and arrested everyone on thepremises. Not only that, but Judge John H Lyle instigated a procedure whereby known gang members were arrested on sight, charged with vagrancy and held in jail at the highest possible bail. Many found themselves unexpectedly accountable on old charges that had been left to drift in the heyday of 'Big Bill' Thompson's reign.

Thus, a lot of mobsters were out of commission, and a lot of expensive damage was inflicted by the raiders. In combination with Eliot Ness and his men, they were costing Capone, Moran and other underworld figures a lot of money, and a lot of time. Investigations in the Lingle case eventually led to a petty hood named Leo Vincent Brothers, who received a 14 year prison sentence, since no one had actually seen him shoot Lingle.

It was a confusing trial, and when the verdict was brought in on 2 April 1931, there were many who believed that Brothers had simply taken a 'dive,' covering up for other mobsters.

Testimony, of a sort, then came from an unexpected source. Mike 'de Pike' Heitler was receiving steadily decreasing preferential treatment in the Capone mob. An aging whoremaster, he finally enacted his resentment in an anonymous letter to Illinois State's Attorney John A Swanson, disclosing all he knew about Capone's bordellos. Capone somehow obtained the letter, and since Heitler was the only one who could have known so much, told Mike 'de Pike' that he was 'through.'

Heitler then wrote a second letter, and told his daughter to dispatch it to the authorities should he die a sudden and unnatural death. He was in fact murdered on 29 April, and his daughter did as he asked. The letter was considerably detailed, and implicated eight Capone mobsters in the Lingle murder. It also quoted Capone as saying that Lingle was a double crosser, and saying 'Jake [Lingle] is going to get his.'

The letter was not substantiated, and would have been weak as evidence in a court of law, but it was yet further grist for the increasing clamor to 'get Capone.' Capone fought back by conducting a 'Capone as Robin Hood' publicity campaign. He set up a soup kitchen for the increasing numbers of Depression-era jobless, he contributed to every charity that had a public enough face to do him good and bought civic groups and Boy Scout troops tickets to sports events.

Ness and his men, dubbed 'The Untouchables' for their resistance to the mob's repeated attempts to bribe and threaten them, continued their activity, aided by the use of a 10-ton flatbed truck with a huge steel ram mounted to the front of it. The truck was efficient at smashing through the steel doors that often protected bootlegging warehouses.

For Capone, 'public relations' was camouflage. He was becoming known as a blight on society, so he sought good publicity by opening a soup kitchen (at right) for victims of the Depression.

Their success was not without its price, however. Capone gunman Frank Picchi was sent to kill Eliot Ness. For days and nights, Picchi stalked Ness. Aware of this activity, Ness moved from his parents' house in the suburbs of Chicago, stopped seeing his girlfriend for the duration, and slept nights in a windowless rented room. Then he and his driver, Frank Basile, were tooling toward the office one morning when they noticed Picchi following them.

Speeding up and rounding a corner, they broadsided their car across an alley. Picchi followed, and forced to stop his car, was seized and knocked cold by Ness. Picchi was remanded to police custody.

Not long after, Frank Basile disappeared. He was found later that day, slain by a mob gunman. Through an informant known as 'The Clown,' Ness and his men tracked down Tony Napoli, the assassin of their man Basile. 'The Clown' had liked Basile, as Basile had always treated him with the respect due another human being, despite the little informant's badly deformed body, which had gained for him the cruel epithet by which he was named by the mob.

Tony Napoli was easily captured, but committed suicide in his jail cell, rather than testify against Capone. Ness, undaunted by the deaths of his friend and his witness, determined to show Capone that he and his men would not be cowed by violence or threats. Since the many trucks he and his men had confiscated had to be moved from their old warehouse to a new one, Ness arranged a parade of trucks — to be routed past Capone's headquarters, at precisely the time that 'The Big Fellow' would be there.

Therefore, Eliot Ness, his men and several squads of Chicago policemen gave the people of Chicago a shot of courage when they drove the 45 trucks, confiscated from Capone breweries, past the Hotel Lexington. They made sure with a phone call that Capone would be watching, and Capone gangsters thronged the steps in front of the hotel, expressing states of rage and amazement, and if one looked carefully enough, 'Snorky' Capone himself could be seen standing at an upstairs window, gnashing his teeth at the spectacle below.

Judge Lyle came up with a plan to arrest Capone on a vagrancy warrant. Vagrancy was a charge that applied when an individual could not list a legitimate source of income, and was seen to be involved in any way with criminal activities. This would serve the function of forcing Capone to tell how he stayed alive if he had no legitimate income, and perhaps, it would open a few cracks in his wall of protection.

Capone once again fled to Florida, only to be told that he was not welcome in Dade County. Since no formal charges had been brought to justify the eviction, Capone's lawyer in Florida, Vincent Giblin, brought suit for the 'harassment' to cease. Capone, feeling that he could, if necessary, establish a permanent base in Florida, answered Judge Lyle's warrant, saying that he would surrender on the vagrancy charge. Not only that, he offered to quit labor racketeering and leave Chicago, provided he could operate his other rackets by 'remote control.'

His offer was turned down, with Chicago Chief Justice McGoorty saying, 'The time has come when the public must choose between the rule of the gangster and the rule of law.'

Meanwhile, Wilson had come up with the first real break in the IRS case against Capone. He and assistants Tessem and Hodges had examined approximately 1.7 million items that they'd accumulated in checking bank records, raids on Capone gambling houses and other receipts from Capone Gang operations.

In the summer of 1930, at the end of yet another long day of peering through reams of paper for a hint or a clue, Wilson stumbled across three black ledgers that had somehow been overlooked: they were the ledgers seized in the Hawthorne Smoke Shop Raid of 1926. They showed net profits of more than $500,000 in an 18-month period between 1924–26. Every few pages, totals were taken and divided among 'A' (for Al); 'R' (for Ralph Capone); 'J' (for Jake Guzik) and so on.

Through painstaking handwriting comparisons between the ledgers and the receipts that they had collected in thousands of file folders, it was determined that one of the authors of the ledgers was Leslie Albert 'Lou' Shumway, who had preceded Fred Ries as a Capone gambling cashier. Unfortunately, Shumway was not to be found.

Also, in 1930–31, Wilson made the acquaintance of St Louis lawyer and dog racing track operator Edward O'Hare. O'Hare knew plenty about Capone's operations, and was willing to help put Capone behind bars, in exchange for help in getting his own son into the US Naval Academy. He verified that more than half of the mob's gambling revenues went into Capone's own till.

In a hurried phone call some months later, O'Hare also warned Wilson of Capone's plot to have him, Patrick Roche, US Attorney George EQ Johnson and Illinois Tax Intelligence Chief Arthur Madden killed by hired gunmen from

At right: **Capone during a break in his trial.** *Below:* **Robert De Niro as Capone in the Paramount movie,** *The Untouchables*.

New York. Wilson and his wife left the Sheridan Plaza Hotel, telling the desk attendant that they were going to Kansas, feigned a drive to Union Station and immediately circled around to the Palmer House Hotel.

A 24-hour guard team was assigned to each intended victim. Investigator Roche told his detectives to bring in Capone, but informants in the police department warned Capone, and he escaped capture. Knowing that Johnny Torrio was in town, Roche parlayed a message through him to Capone: 'If those hoods aren't out of town tonight, I'm going after them myself with two guns.'

Capone called off the killing. Shortly after this bit of excitement, O'Hare had another important message for Wilson: He had located Shumway, the cashier, at a dog track in Florida. Wilson flew to Florida and presented the horrified Shumway with one of two alternatives: either publicly receive a subpoena, and risk death at the hands of the mob, or come and sing quietly, and get the same protection as his fellow 'bookie,' Fred Ries. Shumway accepted the latter course.

Capone meanwhile came to trial on Judge Lyle's vagrancy warrant. His lawyers cannily waited until Lyle was caught up in another case, and made sure that a 'friendly' judge dismissed the warrant. It would not, however, be the same story for the income tax case.

Before Wilson transferred Shumway to a safe hiding place, a federal grand jury secretly convened to hear his testimony. He confirmed that Capone was the head of the gambling operations, and had received net incoming totaling $123,102 for the period covered by the ledgers, for a tax liability in the same period of $32,488. Haste was of the essence in trying the case, however, as offenses committed in 1924 would be barred by the Statute of Limitations from prosecution after 15 March 1931. The grand jury returned an indictment 'in the nick of time' on 13 March 1931.

This was all kept secret until an investigation on tax years 1925–29 could be completed. When this investigation was complete, the grand jury convened publicly, to return another indictment on Capone's tax evasion for those years. The government had been able to piece together a fraction of Capone's income in that period. It amounted to $1,038,655, for a tax liability of $219,260, with penalties of over $160,000.

A week later, the grand jury returned another indictment based on Eliot Ness and 'The Untouchables' raids on Capone's bootlegging industry. This indictment charged Capone and 68 members of his gang with 5000 separate offenses relating to the Volstead Act, and listed violations of Prohibition dating back to Capone's first purchase of a beer truck from Johnny Torrio in 1924.

Ironically for Capone, 1931 was also the year that Lucky Luciano became the king of mobsters in the United States, upon the slaying of the old Mafia Dons Masseria and Maranzano. This is further discussed in the Lucky Luciano segment of this text. Luciano, of course, had cut his old pal Al 'Snorky' Capone in for a major share of the tremendously lucrative 'syndication' of American organized crime.

Instead of seeing a vast, untrammeled future of illegal profit stretching before him, Capone found himself facing a potential 34 years in federal penitentiaries. His lawyers, Thomas Nash and Michael Ahern, approached the prosecution with an offer that Capone would plead guilty in return for a light sentence.

US Attorney Johnson conferred with his fellow prosecutors, and finally said that he would recommend a sentence of two and one-half years, based on various factors—a separate statute of limitations for some tax cases that set the limit at three years; the fact that mob witnesses did not have a high survival rate, etcetera—which seemed to weaken the possibilities of guilty verdicts on all three indictments.

A dapper and cheerful Al Capone and his legal counsel walked into the courtroom on 16 June and entered a plea of guilty. Judge James H Wilkerson then adjourned the court until 30 June. The popular press, sure it was going to be another 'walkover' by the mob, were outraged at what they felt to be yet another defeat: '...a devastating criticism of our legal system.'

On the 30th, Capone and counsel waited lightheartedly for the sentencing. Two and one-half years, with time off for good behavior, would not amount to much more than Capone's old weapons charge, and besides, he could still run things from 'inside.'

The sentencing never came. Instead, Judge Wilkerson said 'The parties to a criminal case may not stipulate as to the judgement to be entered....It is time for somebody to impress upon the defendant that it is utterly impossible to bargain with a federal court.'

Capone was allowed to withdraw his guilty plea, and the trial was scheduled for October. Capone, through the channels of corruption, obtained a list of prospective jurors for his case, and proceeded to bribe and/or threaten them. His face registered shock on 6 October, the first day of jury selection, when it became apparent that Judge Wilkerson—aware of Capone's activities, had switched panels of pros-

At right: **From the *Chicago Evening American* of 6 June 1931.** *Below:* **Robert Stack as Eliot Ness in ABC television's *The Untouchables*. Capone's estate failed in a suit against the series.**

CHICAGO EVENING AMERICAN —Chicago's Most Widely Read Evening Paper—

CAPONE FACES EARLY TRIAL

Early trial as an alleged income tax dodger faced Al Capone, czar of the Midwest rum racket, today as the consequence of his indictment for failure to give the government a "cut" of his illegal profits.

Capone, who went through the formality of surrendering himself yesterday, was at liberty on $50,000 bond. He is charged with evading income tax payments aggregating $215,080 on an alleged six-year income totaling $1,038,654 for the years 1924 to 1929 inclusive.

Conferring today, Assistant District Attorneys Green, Clawson and Grossman declared they were ready for early trial, probably within the next week, adding:

"We want to proceed at the earliest time possible, and we think that will be soon. We have an air-tight case and we want to clinch it."

75 WITNESSES TESTIFY.

They conferred with A. P. Madden, chief of special intelligence unit, of the internal revenue department, on evidence to be expected from seventy-five witnesses who testified before the grand jury. The majority of those witnesses will be summoned at the trial, the prosecutors said.

The sole occasion for delay of even a few days, the attorneys said, is the time required to check and recheck the voluminous indictment to make sure it is unassailable against attack by Capone's attorneys.

HINT PLEA OF GUILTY?

The government attorneys disclaimed any knowledge of rumors about the Federal Building that Capone's attorneys are negotiating for a plea of guilty and acceptance of a heavy fine, as well as payment of the government's due bill for taxes. They profess an utter lack of interest in any such proposal.

Flanked by his attorneys, Capt. William F. Waugh and John J. Goshkin, he surrendered to United States Marshal H. C. W. Laubenheimer late yesterday afternoon immediately after he learned he had been indicted. Date for his arraignment has not been set.

[illegible]PT CHARGE PENDS.

While the government is prepared for most vigorous prosecution of the [illegible], attorneys conceded there is a possibility Capone, who is facing a [illegible] attack, may be called to reckoning on a six [illegible] jail sentence for contempt of court before trial on the income tax charge. In view of the government's haste to try him, that is hardly probable, however.

Capone is on $5,000 bail on an ap[illegible] a six months' jail sentence imposed by Federal Judge James H. Wilkerson for feigning illness when [illegible] before the United States grand jury more than a [illegible]

In U. S. Tax Net

Al Capone, snapped as he left the Federal Building where he signed a $50,000 bond on an indictment charging he defrauded Uncle Sam of income tax.

Evening American photo.

COOPER SMILES WORTH CASH!

Hey, kids! Say it with a smile!

Youngsters smile a good deal of the time—and that's why the Chicago Evening American in conjunction with the RKO State-Lake Theater is announcing a Smile Hunt.

The boy-actor Jackie Cooper is the inspiration. No doubt you saw him in "Skippy" and agreed with the movie-makers that he's the best child actor on the screen. Perhaps you have already seen him with Richard Dix in "Donovan's Kid," at the State-Lake Theater.

PAYS TO SMILE.

In both productions Jackie ("Skippy") Cooper said it with a smile. That's why the Smile-Hunt Man is combing Chicago to find boys and girls who can smile like Jackie does. It always pays to say it with a smile—but for the next few days it will pay double.

Here's why—and how! The Smile-Hunt man will have a camera with him. He's going to take pictures of boys and girls in schools, playgrounds, in parks, in street-crowds—anywhere that he can find smiling boys and girls. When the pictures are made he'll hunt through them and circle the six boys or girls whose smile is most like Jackie Cooper's.

The best Cooper Smile will be awarded a $5 gold piece every day. The next five best smiles daily will be presented with guest tickets to see Jackie Cooper and his "big brudder" Richard Dix in "Donovan's Kid" at the State-Lake Theater.

So keep smiling, Kids, especially if you see the Smile-Hunt Man with his camera. Look in The Evening American Monday for the first picture. If your smile is circled come to Room 825 Hearst Building, 326 W. Madison st. and claim the reward. The best smile—the one that wins the gold piece—will have a double ring around it. The other smiles winning guests tickets will just have one ring around them.

$5 Smiles!

Smile doublers for Jackie ("Skippy") Cooper (above) should watch Monday's Evening American for awards.

ALCOCK DRAFTS NEW SHAKEUP

Another widespread police shake-up was presaged today by Commissioner John H. Alcock.

The commissioner said today he would devote the week end to "working on a big transfer order." Further than that he would not reveal, but it was intimated that in order he would establish a new gambling squad under command of Capt. O'Connor.

Meanwhile, Capt. Daniel Gilbert of the Wabash av. station, set about today with a clean slate to "clean up" his district on orders [illegible] the commissioner coincident [illegible] the most sweeping shakeup ever dealt a single police district.

Effective today, every man of the Wabash av. station was transferred and replaced by 192 policemen and sergeants from various other districts throughout the city. The commissioner particularly wants vice and gambling wiped out of Capt. Gilbert's district, he told the station commander.

WORLD PROTEST [illegible]

His Holiness Plans Drastic Action in War With Italy.

BY GUGLIELMO EMANUEL, International News Service Staff Correspondent.

ROME, June 6. — A solemn protest to the world may soon be made by Pope Pius XI, if the Italian government fails to answer the Vatican's series of notes regarding Fascist activity against Catholic young peoples' organizations, it was rumored here today.

Just what form the protest might take could not be learned. Of recent months, his holiness has made wide use of the radio to address Catholics throughout the world, the last occasion being his address on the anniversary of the famous "Rerum Novarum" encyclical of Pope Leo XIII.

HAS SENT 2 NOTES.

Two notes have been sent by the Vatican to the Fascist government, protesting against the dissolution of Catholic youth organizations and asking apologies and reparations for alleged attacks by Fascists against church property.

Neither of these [illegible] answered. Yesterday the [illegible] ficial Vatican newspaper [illegible] tore Romano published an [illegible] statement calling upon the [illegible] government to [illegible] charge that the [illegible] nation-wide organization [illegible] lic youth, had participated [illegible] litical affairs.

ALLUDES TO CONFLICT.

His holiness alluded to the conflict in speaking to eighty Catholics from Milan who were received in audience at the Vatican. He said:

"We are passing through a period of great sorrow. But we have the consolation of defending justice and waging a battle for liberty of conscience and the spiritual welfare of all.

"Sorrow is being caused by the hand of man, but consolation is administered by the hand of God. We have a physical feeling that God is with us."

Although it was reported yesterday that the Pope had spurned a compromise offer that the women's Catholic clubs be reopened, leaving the men's associations in their present state, no official confirmation could be obtained.

[illegible]

Dies [illegible]

Henry Bowl[illegible] st., a carpet [illegible] died of heart [illegible] ing a rug in [illegible] Heellem, 5806 [illegible]

CLEAR KELLY IN SANITARY CASE

Edward J. Kelly, president of the South Park commission and chief engineer for the Sanitary District, today received the congratulations of friends upon his complete vindication of complicity in the allegedly illegal Sanitary District expenditures.

He was cleared of all charges when the grand jury, which late last night re-indicted Timothy J. Crowe and eight other trustees and officials of the district, refused to name Engineer Kelly in a true bill.

The grand jury made a searching inquiry into the charges against the chief engineer of the district and despite the attempts of Assistant State's Attorney John E. Northup to obtain an indictment the jurors held that there was no evidence involving him in any violation of the law.

Those named with Crowe in the new indictments are [illegible] M. Whalen, John J. [illegible], Frank J. Link, John K. Lawle[illegible], August Miller, former trustee [illegible] John T. Millen, Timothy Co[illegible] [illegible]ar-ton Edelstein [illegible] of the dis[illegible] a fug[illegible]

TEACHERS WAIT SCRIP RULING

A proposal for payment of $5,200,000 in salaries overdue to school teachers and other employes of the Board of Education, in the form of interest bearing certificates will be acted upon by the board Wednesday, it was announced today.

President Lewis E. Myers announced that attorneys had been instructed to draw up necessary papers. The plan provides that tax anticipation warrants to the amount of the salaries due be placed in trust. Against the trust interest bearing certificates will be issued. These may be accepted as credits by merchants.

MANY IN DIRE NEED

Regarding the plan Mr. Myers said:

"I have received reports to the effect that many employes of the school system are in desperate need of financial aid. So far as I can see the plan to issue scrip is the only feasible one to meet the present situation."

Employes will not [illegible] the scrip in lieu [illegible] checks unless they wish [illegible]

[illegible]

GREYHOUND, 9 OASES LOCKED

Ten widely scattered oases in the Chicago area were padlocked today by order of Federal Judge Charles E. Woodward on orders enforcing permanent injunctions against the speakeasies.

The Greyhound Roadhouse, widely known night club on the Desplaines River at River road in the township of Leyden, was the principal place padlocked. Agents raided it some time ago and found a great supply of assorted liquors. It is owned by Nick DeGracio and Tony St. Lucia.

A lodge hall and saloon which had operated for forty years at 2110 N. Damen av., was another "spot" padlocked. It was owned by Walter Poklacki. His attorneys appealed the case for him.

DENTIST KILLED SELF, VERDICT

A verdict of "suicide while temporarily insane due to financial difficulties" was returned today by a coroner's jury in the death of Dr. James D. Frankel, 4[illegible], 1164 N. Dearborn st., a dentist. He shot himself to death last night.

A note found in the apartment where the doctor had taken his life was the foundation for the verdict. It read:

"I see no other way. Life seems impossible. I am sorry for all the trouble this will cause my family and friends. I've been putting this off from day to day. I don't take any stock in Sir Conan Doyle's spiritual messages after life, but if it's true, you'll hear from me soon."

Dr. Henry A. Frankel, brother of the dead man, also a dentist with offices in the Pittfield Building, 55 E. Washington st., told the jury that his brother had been despondent over stock losses and the depreciation of his real estate holdings.

The body was found in the doctor's apartment by Mrs. Susanne [illegible]man, 5133 Kenmore av., who had called to see him with regard [illegible] apartment.

The dead man was unmarried.

DIES IN PLUNGE FROM WINDOW

Leaping or falling out of a third story window at 730 N. Wells st., Secondo Guidarelli, [illegible], head of S. [illegible] & Sons, [illegible] killed today. His death was blamed indirectly [illegible] his son on [illegible]quences of a beating administered by bandits three weeks ago.

A[illegible] Macio, who lived with his father over the [illegible] establishment at Superior [illegible] discovered his [illegible] sidewalk [illegible] floor bedroom [illegible]

[illegible]

3-MONTH [illegible] CONTRACT GIVEN ONLY 1 MONTH LEFT

[illegible]

DE-RACIALZED WORLD, PRICE OF PEACE, HE SAYS

ABERDEEN, Scotland, June 6 (By International News Service.) The price of world peace is a uni-tribal de-racialized world produced through the intermarriage of the black, yellow and white races, Sir Arthur Keith, noted British biologist, declared in his rectorial address at Aberdeen University today.

MAN LEAPS FROM EIGHTH FLOOR OF HOTEL, LIVES

KANSAS CITY, June 6.—(By International News Service.)—Having leaped eight floors from a room of a downtown hotel here in an effort to end his life, De Ward Cummings, 28, jobless, today lived to tell about it. His condition is critical.

A Great Big Automobile with more than 70 HORSEPOW[ER]

SELLING FOR ONLY $595 to $795 F. O. B. [illegible] Special [illegible]

You will get marvelous satisfaction out of owning *the most powerful of all low-priced cars* — the popular new De Vaux 6-75. Without special fuels, the famous Hall Engine develops more than 70 horsepower and provides performance ability far greater than any car within two hundred dollars of the De Vaux sedan price:—

70 to 80 Miles An Hour, actual miles

5 to 55 Miles An Hour, in only 19 Seconds

Quiet, Smooth High Speeds All Day Long

Sensational Hill-Climbing Power

De Vaux-Hall Motors—an INDEPENDENT COMPANY *— America's Fastest Growing Manufacturer*

NORMAN DE VAUX . . . *successful ma[illegible]*
COL. ELBERT J. HALL . . . *co-designer of Lib[illegible]*

IGNORED CONVENT[IONS]

in designing this exceptional motor ca[r]

— 113-Inch Wheelbase
— 58-Inch Rear Car Tread
— Constant-Mesh Gears
— Quiet Second
— Six-Port Intake Manifold (first time in any L-head passenger-car engine)
— 6-Inch Frame, 2¼-Inch Flange
— Houdaille Hydraulic Shock Absorbers
— 214.7 Cub[ic] Piston Di[splace]ment
— Steeldra[illegible] Wheel Bra[kes]
— Steel-an[illegible] Bodies, In[illegible] Against H[illegible] Cold
— Shackles [illegible] End of Fro[nt illegible]
— 69-Inch [illegible] Height

. . . and many other features characteristi[c illegible] priced cars.

$595 to $795 DeVaux 6

Powered by the Famous HALL ENGINE *with Six-Port Intake*

Come Today!

DISTRIBUTOR
Reo Motor Sales Company
226 Lafayette Blvd., So.
South Bend, Indiana

THE R. H. COLLINS AUTOMOBILE CO.
DISTRIBUTORS
2220 S. MICHIGAN AVENUE CALUMET 6900

[illegible]

MONDAY, JUNE 8th—11 A.M. SHARP

Buy Furs and Furniture at Your Own Price!

PUBLIC AUCTION

Furs and Furniture

Manufacturers going out of business. The Largest Stock of Furs and Furniture liquidation to be sold in Chicago at—

CHARLES W. SILVER & CO. Salesroom
315 W. ADAMS ST. Between Franklin and Market Sts.

THE FURS—consist of Pointed Fox Scarfs, Beige Foxes, Cross Foxes — Sables — Martins—Fur Coats of Mink, Seal, Sealine, Muskrats—also Jacquettes, plain and trimmed. Also dressed skins.

THE FURNITURE—consists of complete sets of Dining Room Furniture—and Dinette Sets—a large assortment of beautiful Bedroom Sets in all colors and woods—artistically finished.

Everything Must Go—Monday, June 8th

CHARLES W. SILVER & CO. Auctioneers
315 W. ADAMS ST. Between Franklin and Market Sts.

Drunkenness Is a Disease!

This FREE Booklet Explains Facts That Every Person Should Know

HERE is an authoritative treatise written on the disease of inebriety and its cure, written especially for the Keeley Institute. It is based on fifty years' experience, embracing the treatment of more than 400,000 patients, including men and women from all walks of life.

It tells you "why" the medical profession recognizes drunkenness as a disease; what famous medical authorities say about the disease of drunkenness . . . and "how" drunkenness can be cured *permanently*. The booklet is free, and mailed in a plain envelope. Write at once for your copy. *NOW!*

Chicago Address:
1255 No. Dearborn St. Phone: Sup. 5300
Address D. M. Nelson, Secretary

KEELEY INSTITUTE

pective jurors with a fellow judge. Capone's efforts had been, happily, in vain.

By the end of that day, the jury was chosen. On 7 October, testimony began. A government clerk testified that Capone filed no income tax returns for the years 1924–29; a witness at a Hawthorne Smoke Shop raid swore that Capone claimed ownership of that vice den; and ex-bookie Shumway testified that the Smoke Shop took in more than $550,000 during his two years of employment as a Capone bookkeeper.

On 8 October, a letter from Capone's lawyer Lawrence P Mattingly was featured in the evidence. The letter, written when the Capone faction realized that the IRS investigation was serious, admitted Capone's non-payment of taxes in an attempt to 'deal' a fine, and to avoid a prison sentence. The letter here served just the opposite of its intended purpose. Lawyer Albert Fink attempted then to justify non-payment of tax as a natural human tendency, citing the Boston Tea Party: the judge indicated that the trial is a 'tea party' of another kind. That night, Frankie Rio told Capone that he ought to be buying a suit with stripes, for he was surely going to prison. Capone retorted, 'The hell I am!'

Phil D'Andrea had been in the custom of sitting just behind Capone and his counsel, fixing jurors with a cold, murderous look. On Friday, 9 October, D'Andrea had his effect. A spate of Florida witnesses testified concerning Western Union money orders received by Capone at Palm Island: a small fortune was traceable to Capone. Finally, John Fotre, the Western Union agent who transmitted most of the money orders in the Hotel Lexington, balked in testimony, suddenly denying any knowledge of the case.

When Judge Wilkerson reproved the witness after that day's trial session, Fotre replied, 'What can you expect, when they let one of Capone's hoodlums sit there with his hand on his gun?' On 10 October, two IRS agents followed D'Andrea into a crowded elevator. One brushed up against him to 'feel' for the gun in its shoulder holster. They then reported to Judge Wilkerson, who told them that they had to 'grab' D'Andrea outside of the courtroom.

Trial in session once more, D'Andrea got a note that a telegram had arrived for him, and as he left the courtroom, the agents apprehended him turn him over to the police. D'Andrea flashed one of the phony 'sheriff's deputy' cards that Capone supplied his mobsters, to circumvent prosecution on weapons charges.

The judge found D'Andrea guilty of contempt of court and sent him to prison for six months. Then followed a procession of witnesses who had mercantile interactions with Capone: this took up two days, and firmly demonstrated that Al 'Snorky' Capone's spending habits were concomitant with his having been a wealthy man.

On 13 October, a former IRS agent testified to Capone's speakeasy operation at the Hawthorne Smokeshop, and Judge Wilkerson demanded that Capone be referred to by his defense counsel as 'the defendant,' and not as 'Al.'

It was at about this time that the popular press took up the habit of freely calling Al Capone by a name that he hated: 'Scarface.' In fact, he would come to be known coast-to-coast—and around the world—not as 'Snorky,' but as 'Scarface'—'Scarface' Al Capone.

On 14 October, Fred Ries implicated Pete Penovich, Frank Pope, Jake Guzik, Ralph Capone and Jimmy Mondi in the affairs of the Hawthorne Smoke Shop. Capone's lawyers were shaky, but not Capone: he paid Fink and Ahern so much that

he felt they couldn't possibly lose the case for him. On 15 October, defense testimony began.

The defense attempted to prove that Capone lost so much at gambling that he exhausted his income as fast as he made it. Since none of the racetrack bookies and other gambling accountants seem to have kept exact records, their testimony was inadmissible: besides, deduction of gambling losses from one's taxes was only allowed if those losses came out of money that had been *won* by gambling.

The defense collapsed. Johnny Torrio, expected to be called up as Capone's 'employer' during the tax periods in question, was not called upon. It was clear then that Al Capone was going to prison. Still, on 16 October, the defense stridently declared, in its summary, that Capone was a persecuted figure, and that the 'only sin' he had ever committed was that of being a spendthrift.

On 17 October, prosecutor George EQ Johnson rebuffed the defense summary. He also attacked Capone's status as a modern day 'Robin Hood,' pointing out that Capone's earnings went toward buying an immense wardrobe, buying his Palm Island estate, buying favored friends diamond-studded belt buckles and other extravagances. Judge Wilkerson then explained the principles underlying the charges against Capone to the jury, who then retired for deliberation.

At 11 o'clock that evening, Capone was called to come to the courtroom to hear the jurors' verdict. Capone was found guilty on three counts of tax evasion and two counts of failing to file a return. Sentencing was scheduled for 24 October.

Capone was sentenced, altogether, to 11 years in prison, with fines totalling $50,000 and court costs totalling $30,000. Everyone in the country was surprised that Fink and Ahern hadn't attacked the government's case on its shaky Statute of Limitations footing. This failure eventually cost Fink and Ahern their gangster clientele.

Capone was settled in the Cook County Jail, pending an appeal. He was allowed to have business conferences there, and essentially was given preferential treatment. The government, upon being informed of Capone's favored status in that institution, demanded his transfer to the prison's hospital ward, with a special, heavy guard on 27 February 1932.

His appeal was denied, and Capone was transferred to Atlanta Federal Penitentiary on 4 May 1932. His mother retained William Leahy, one of the best lawyers in the US, to petition for a retrial on the basis of the Statute of Limitations.

During the processing of this latest appeal, the very source of much of Capone's criminal income dried up: Prohibition was repealed on 5 December 1933. In January 1934, Capone appeared in federal court to hear the outcome of his lawyer's petition. It was ruled that a defendant could not count time spent outside of the jurisdiction in which he committed his offenses as applicable to the Statute of Limitations. Therefore, the time spent in Florida didn't count for Chicago income, and vice versa: and the early tax evasion charges held.

The federal government had meanwhile been contemplating building a maximum security prison for the country's most dangerous criminals on Alcatraz Island, site of an abandoned US Army base in San Francisco Bay. In January, 1934, Capone was tipped off that he was the 'star attraction' among prisoners slated for the new facility.

Above right: Mug shots of Al Capone from 1931. *At right:* Alcatraz as seen from the city of San Francisco. See text, this page.

In August, 1934, a high-security prison train took Al Capone and numerous other 'incorrigibles' across the continent to the cold, hard 'Rock' in San Francisco Bay. Less than a year after Capone's arrival at Alcatraz, 'Machine Gun' Jack McGurn was shot to death in a Chicago bowling alley, on St Valentine's Day, 1935, in obvious retribution for the St Valentine's Day Massacre of 1929.

On 5 February 1938, Capone began to manifest symptoms of advanced syphillitic disorder. He had moments of blank staring, loss of motor control and babbling, intermixed with lucidity. In the prison infirmary, the seriousness of his disease was made clear to him.

Not long after, the Reverend Silas Thweat visited Alcatraz to conduct a Sunday service. Reverend Thweat asked if any of them felt in need of prayer. Capone, a shaken man, raised his hand. The Reverend then asked if any of them felt the need for a personal saviour, and would they stand up and confess the fact before their fellows? Capone stood up and confessed.

Alphonse Capone rapidly deteriorated in his syphilitic condition. He very shortly became an individual whose mental state was no longer conducive to any activity, criminal or legal, and was confined for continuous treatment in the prison infirmary. His sentence had been reduced for good behavior, and, considering his extreme illness, the authorities released him from Alcatraz on 6 January 1939, for transfer to Terminal Island Federal Correctional Institution, near Los Angeles.

He still had a few months to serve on a 'failure to file tax returns' misdemeanor charge. Finally, on 16 November 1939, his sentence served and fines paid off at last, he was released. He and Mae, his wife, stayed until springtime in the vicinity of Baltimore's Union Memorial Hospital, where Capone underwent treatment by a Dr Joseph Moore, a renowned syphilologist.

He spent the remainder of his life as an addled paralytic. Constantly beset by fears that he was being hunted by rival mobsters, his home became a place of seclusion.

Al Capone died on 25 January 1947, the victim of a brain hemorrhage. He was buried in Chicago's Mount Olivet Cemetery. The service was small, without full rites as the Catholic Church could not condone Capone's criminal life. Still, he was buried in consecrated ground, as it was felt that Alphonse Capone had truly repented, albeit under duress of a terrible disease.

The 1950s saw the deaths by natural causes of Sam Hunt, Terry Druggan, Phil D'Andrea, Jake Guzik and Louis 'Little New York' Campagna. Johnny Torrio died naturally, of a coronary in a New York barbershop. Bugs Moran, serving a 10-year sentence for bank robbery, called for a priest and gave a full confession before his death a month or so later of lung cancer.

Eliot Ness, who had been instrumental in bringing about Capone's incarceration, went on to break up more bootlegging operations in Kentucky, Tennessee and Ohio. He then conducted a six-year cleanup of the Cleveland, Ohio Police Department that resulted in 200 resignations, and prison sentences for a dozen high police officials. During this same period, Ness instituted the Cleveland Police Academy and founded Cleveland's Boys Town.

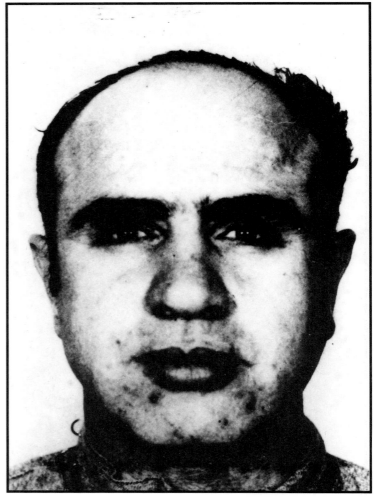

He won the US Navy's Meritorious Service Citation for his work in the Federal Security Agency during World War II, and finally settled down to his own business, in Coudersport, Pennsylvania after the war. As President of the Guaranty Paper Corporation and Fidelity Check Corporation, he led a quiet life with his wife Betty and their son, Bobby. Eliot Ness, one of the nation's legendary crime fighters, died of a heart attack on 16 May 1957.

Red Rudensky, a safecracker who had shared a cell with Capone in Atlanta Federal Penitentiary, founded the prison paper *The Atlantian*. After 35 years behind bars, Rudensky was freed to become chief copy editor for the St Paul Advertising Agency, proof positive that a gangster can lead a reformed life.

Al Capone died a penniless man.

Below far left: A pro-FBI, 1930s cartoon. *Below:* Capone's boat arrives at Alcatraz, 1934. *Below left:* A sick Al Capone, near the end of his term. *At right:* Ness' answer to street life (see text).

Lucky Luciano and His Underworld

He was born Salvatore Lucania in the tiny hillside village of Lercara Friddi, Sicily. The third of five children born to Antonio and Rosalie Lucania, he was his mother's favorite of all the children, and this eviscerated his father's discipline that the boy follow in his own hard-working but poor footsteps.

The family scrimped and saved to come to the 'promised land' of America, and only achieved that dream when a cousin loaned them the amount they were lacking—and was paid back within two years. In April 1906, the Lucanias set off for America aboard a decrepit old steamship. They went steerage class, below decks, and when they emerged in America, they encountered a world that was wildly different than anything they had ever seen in tiny Lercara Friddi.

Instead of being the land of gold it was held out to be, America was a place of even more toil and privation than they had known in poverty-stricken Sicily. At least, there they had 'room to move,' but on Manhattan's Lower East Side, their tiny, dark tenement was crowded together with other tiny, dark tenements—and while the pay was higher than in Sicily, here the work of the menial laborer was seen as without honor, and everything was toweringly expensive.

Their neighborhood was a melting pot of Sicilians, Calabrians, Irish and Jews. The schools, as opposed to those in Italy, were free, and the Lucanias saw great hope for their children in that. Their children, though, had a tough time learning their lessons in English. While his siblings applied themselves and struggled with the problem, overcoming it

eventually, young Salvatore rebelled and turned in belligerence to the street life of boy gangs.

His frequent truancy resulted, finally, in his being remanded to the Brooklyn Truant School in 1911, for a stay of four months. Both his mother and father insisted on his finishing school or getting a job. However, Salvatore learned his lessons far more readily from the thieves and loan sharks in his neighborhood, and himself became a thief; also, because of the distinction of having been 'sent up' for his truancy, he was admired by other budding hoodlums, and became the leader of a gang of young thieves and muggers.

In the five years of his public schooling, he had perceived that some of the smartest kids in his classes had been Jews and members of mainland Italian bloodlines: this was to result in his seeking partnerships with mobsters of ethnic persuasions that went beyond the Mafia's strictly Sicilian tradition. In turn, these associations were to affect his relations with the old Mafia Dons who would seek, years later, to control him and his gang.

Even as a boy, he was adept at organizing his gang so that their profits were pooled and carefully doled out to the members—to avoid detection by their parents (and by beat cops), who would surely note any sudden extravagance.

Soon, his gang and others like it outgrew the Lower East Side, and started encroaching on the 'no man's land' of central Manhattan. While conflicts and some bloodshed resulted, midtown was also a place where new alliances could be struck. A neutral zone for gangs was the Victoria Movie Theater. In fact, Salvatore met Francesco Castiglia there. While Francesco was a Calabrian, and not a fellow Sicilian, Castiglia (later known as 'Frank Costello') proved to have the intelligence that Salvatore had previously attributed only to Jews. A lifelong friendship in crime was the result of this meeting.

Salvatore's legitimate job—a coverup for the increasing amounts of money he made as a criminal (he was by now 15 or 16)—was as a delivery boy for a women's haberdasher, the Goodman Hat Company. Max Goodman paid the young Sicilian more than the going rate, and took him under his wing. Salvatore relished this introduction to genteel culture; still, he continued his plunge into the world of crime. He became a drug courier for George Scanlon, a wealthy gangster who had pioneered the gutter industry of drug pushing.

He was caught some months later with a vial of heroin: it was tucked into a Goodman's package he was carrying, and was meant for a customer en route to the lady whose hat he was obviously carrying. On 26 June 1916, he was sentenced to one year at Hampton Farms Penitentiary. What happened next is ironic in that it shows he could have gone straight if he'd have had the will power. Mr Goodman chided him, and Salvatore resolved to be a model prisoner. Succeeding in this determination, he was released in six months.

He was now 'Charlie' Lucania, as he hated the name Salvatore—he felt its diminutive, the familiar 'Sal,' was a girl's name. Free again, he took up his old habits, and his father, exasperated threw him out of the house. He was nineteen, and while some of his gang members took opportunities to go straight, Charlie Lucania never wanted to become a 'crumb,' which is what he called people who worked for a

The Statue of Liberty *(at left and right)* **welcomed the Lucanias to New York Harbor in 1906. Ironically, young Salvatore was to recreate the very enslavements his parents fled.**

living. He soon met up with the then-young Meyer Lansky and Benny 'Bugsy' Siegel: both would turn out to be important in Lucania's future.

So, as of 1917, the nucleus of what was to become an all-pervasive, nationwide menace had been formed: Lucania, Costello, Lansky and Siegel. By the end of 1919, they had a gang of 20 members, robbing small banks, warehouses and stores in Manhattan and East Harlem. Roaming like jackals, they blazed a violent path to criminal success.

They soon branched out into bookmaking, and equally soon learned the ways of buying influence, setting up what they called a 'Buy-Money Bank,' whose chief executive officer was Frank Costello. They also quickly moved into gambling—a beginning that would become a nationwide empire within two decades. Then, on 27 October 1919, an event happened that promised even greater illegal profits.

Congress passed the Volstead Act, which effectively opened the Prohibition Era. News from Chicago via a 'local boy made good,' Al Capone, a petty thug before being tapped for duty in Chicago by gangster Johnny Torrio, told a tale of garnering tremendous power and profit through bootlegging.

Shortly thereafter, an acquaintance named Joe Adonis needed Lucania's help with a shipment of illegal booze. Dealing through Philadelphia's Irving Wexler, also known as 'Waxey Gordon,' Adonis and Lucania struck a deal that was to make them all rich—and break Lucania's gang into the bootlegging racket. It was the first of many deals with Waxey Gordon for Charlie Lucania.

Bootlegging was seen as a 'victimless crime,' and some unscrupulous police were easily persuaded, with influence payments, to ignore Lucania's activities. The gang's profits, and influence, tripled when they began to apply Meyer Lansky's supply-and-demand formulation: buy the best, don't cut it, and sell at premium prices to the highest social classes buying—therein lay a diabolical economy of making money and gaining support at the levels of society where it would do the outlaws the most good.

They concentrated their bootlegging efforts on Scotch whiskey. Also, by that time, their operations had gotten so big that the various gang members had to specialize. Lucania was the executive overseer of the organization, also handling recruitment and alliances with other gangs; Costello was in charge of gambling and influence payments; Lansky

As youths, these men linked up with 'Charlie' Lucania/Luciano: Frank Costello *(below)*; **'Bugsy' Siegel** *(at bottom)*; **and Meyer Lansky** *(below left)*. *At right:* **A twentieth-century tenement.**

and Siegel formed the 'Bug and Meyer Gang,' hijackers and shipment guards, with no job too big or small; and Joe Adonis had charge of a number of rackets.

Lucania soon recruited new members. Vito Genovese, a tough little Neapolitan, and — as Lucania found out later — eventually Lucania's potent enemy; Francesco Chiccio Scalese, or 'Frankie Cheech,' a vital connection to the gangs of Brooklyn, who himself recruited Carlo Gambino (destined to become an extremely powerful mobster); and Albert Anastasia, a ruthless killer who had just recently been released from Sing Sing — he was to be Lucania's 'enforcer.'

Lansky brought in notorious strong-arm expert Louis Buchalter, also known as 'Charlie Lepke,' whose protection racket in Manhattan's old Garment District was reorganized for maximum efficiency, and was also used as a way to channel illegal alcohol throughout the district. Frank Costello proposed, and succeeded in forming, an alliance with Dutch Schultz, the Bronx 'King of Beer.' Then, too, came Abner 'Longie' Zwillman and his partner Willie Moretti, two important racketeers in northern New Jersey.

Yet another associate of the gang was a man who had incalculable influence on Lucania—Arnold Rothstein, gambling racketeer and prodigal son of a highly regarded Jewish family. Among the scams attributed to Rothstein was the fixing of the 1919 World Series, which resulted in the infamous 'Black Sox' scandal.

Rothstein got in on bootlegging immediately, with the inception of Prohibition. Travelling to Scotland—and gambling on shipboard all the way—he set up binding contracts with Scotch whiskey distillers that guaranteed delivery to a point just off the New Jersey coast, and just a few feet beyond the US territorial limit. He then went to 'Waxey Gordon' to arrange speedboat pickup and stateside distribution of the cargo.

Sartorially speaking, Rothstein took Lucania under his wing, and taught him how to dress. He also taught him etiquette—for Lucania had a powerful yen to be 'classy.'

Another Lucania associate, Arnold Rothstein, bribed certain of the Chicago White Sox (below) to lose the 1919 World Series.

Rothstein also arranged for Lucania's organization to have first 'dibs' on incoming shipments via 'Waxey.' This was an arrangement that would prove vital to the gang's monetary growth as well as to the range of its territorial influence.

The bootlegging operation did not, however, come off without a hitch: hijackers were making inroads on shipments, and a backup supply was needed. The solution was to cut the whiskey, using grain alcohol, flavoring agents, counterfeit labels and identical bottles in order to simulate the 'real thing.' The real Scotch was sold to important customers for $30 per fifth, and a case of same could cost as high as $1000 if supply was especially low.

Waxey Gordon already controlled a number of grain alcohol distilleries in Philadelphia, and a deal was struck with him. Also, rum runners in the employ of the mob used speedboats to transport illegal grain alcohol from Cuba to the continental US. The gang's importation, distribution and bottling empire soon came to rival that of any major 'above ground' industry.

By 1923 the head of a growing empire and a young man of 26, Lucania attracted the attention of the old Mafia chieftains who had come to America as grown men, and were now totally ripe in their corruption. These men lived entirely in their Italian ghetto empires, and had rackets running that involved most of the ghetto residents' life necessities. They held their fellow immigrants in an iron grip, and extorted every penny they could from them. By way of 'enforcing' their hold on the populace, and to protect themselves from reprisals, they had formidable armies of thugs, numbering in the hundreds usually. They had the people in a state of near-superstitious fear, and had the authorities in their pockets, by means of well-financed appeals to common human greed.

Giuseppe 'Joe the Boss' Masseria, Salvatore Maranzano and Ciro Terranova were the old Mafia Dons that ruled over much of New York and New Jersey, with 'Joe the Boss' being the chief among them, the acknowledged 'Boss of Bosses.' With the advent of Prohibition, they sought to grow out of the ghetto and grab a major share of the booming bootlegging market. On the way, of course, they sought to eliminate competitors. One method of doing this was by way of taking them over; mergers were proposed.

Salvatore Maranzano tendered an offer to Lucania, which Lucania could not accept, as joining forces with the Mafia— a strictly Sicilian organization—would mean dropping all his non-Sicilian associates, such as Genovese, Adonis, Lansky, Siegel and Rothstein—and that would be costly indeed. Lucania refused, and went on with his own operations, confident, but not totally secure, in his partners' firepower, in case of the devastating reprisals that Maranzano was capable of executing.

This last-mentioned destructive ability was tested on almost every alcohol run—hijackers often jumped the convoys, and often men were killed. Also, Lucania had other operations—robbery, burglary and extortion—that required occasional killings. Yet it was all well hidden behind the well-oiled machinery of graft; authorities were pleased to ignore gangland doings as long as payment was made, and 'as long as private citizens are not harmed.' As for this last, the true menace of Lucania's 'machine' would, in time, reveal itself in all its malignancy.

By now, the Lucania organization's alcohol and gambling interests were being given a market boost on the 'Sawdust Trail' of roadhouses that lay just beyond the Jersey Palisades. These roadhouses were gambling dens and speakeasies with sawdust-strewn floors—the easier to dispose of drinks in case of a raid.

He was secure in his reputation as a supplier of the best bootleg booze, and his clientele included the very top echelons of society. Country clubs welcomed him; he became a low-handicap golfer, and played polo on private estates. He had become somewhat of a darling of society. He toured the best nightspots in Manhattan, often with one of the flashy young ladies that self-styled ladies' man Joe Adonis introduced him to.

Some of the seamier aspects of Lucania's operations—like the narcotics trade—were strictly kept secret from the gang's newly-made friends in 'polite society.' Such a 'tightly capped bottle' was destined to burst: Lucania was arrested for possession of several packages of pure heroin on 5 June 1923, and swiftly made a deal to guide the narcotics squad to a large cache in exchange for his freedom.

As a way to buy back badly needed upper class good will, Lucania invested in hundreds of hard-to-get tickets—all seats in the front five rows—for the heavily anticipated Jack Dempsey/Luis Firpo title fight on 14 September 1923. He

Lucania/Luciano shunned honest work, yet sought to be 'classy' on a level concomitant with posh New York hotels like the Biltmore *(below)*, and great edifices like Penn Station *(at right)*.

distributed these tickets to those personages he most needed to win back, which he did successfully.

Maranzano made another proposal that he claimed would put Lucania at the top of the heap, if only Lucania would help him eliminate a nemesis, Ciro Terranova, 'The Artichoke King,' whose cornering of the ghetto greengrocer protection racket had gained him his nickname. Figuring that Maranzano would simply eliminate Terranova and then 'bump off' Lucania himself when the time was ripe, Lucania again declined—a move that added to his gangland reputation as a fearless but extremely canny operator.

It also resulted in similar ovations from such bootleggers as Sam Bronfman, Louis Rosenstiel, Moe Dalitz, Johnny Scalise and Philip and Vincent Mangano. Most importantly, Giuseppe 'Joe the Boss' Masseria, sent a close ally of his to meet Lucania and his associates. The meeting took place at the Lucania headquarters, Manhattan's Claridge Hotel. The man sent to meet them was a close Masseria associate named Gaetano 'Tom' Reina.

This opened the way for a meeting at Jack & Charlie's 21 Club, a popular speakeasy, where Masseria and Lucania and associates, in a celebratory mood, paved the way for a private meeting between the two leaders. At that latter meeting, Masseria made it clear that he expected a war with that hated pretender to his throne, Maranzano. He wanted Lucania's allegiance in order to eliminate Maranzano.

On his part, Lucania was sure that the winner of such a battle would inevitably turn on him, the young thug, the upstart. He himself had, from time to time, considered some of his own confederates expendable. He made up his mind that, if he were to progress in satisfying his own avarice, both of the older mobsters had to be murdered, but he had to bide his time. Luciano rejected the offer, but kept the negotiating door open.

A sudden rash of hijackings cut short Lucania's bootleg alcohol supply, and his organization became desperate. The only recourse for Lucania was to visit 'Nucky' Johnson, the 'King of the Jersey Coast.' It was a meeting that came to involve far more than bootleg alcohol. In exchange for giving Lucania exclusive rights to slot machines, gambling and shipment landings on his coast, including providing protection for same, Johnson was granted 10 percent of all Lucania's bootlegging earnings for the extent of Prohibition. And, Johnson tipped Lucania off to a Maranzano shipment that was coming in the next night. Of course, Lucania hijacked same.

This visit to Johnson opened up so much new territory for him that it put Lucania directly on the path toward becoming the not only the underworld king of Manhattan, but of the entire Eastern Seaboard. If he were to succeed in grabbing Masseria's operations, Lucky Luciano would truly be 'the Boss.' With no retaliation from Maranzano for the hijacking, Lucania's mind was made up: apparently, Maranzano had 'gone soft.' Lucania would go with Masseria, they would overpower Maranzano, and then Lucania would find a way to eliminate Masseria—but there was other work to be done first.

By the mid-1920s, Lucania had acquired wealth, societally acceptable aesthetic sense, and the veneer of a gentleman. Aside from the fact that he had never lost his Lower East Side speech inflection, he always had an air of menace about him. Try as he might to distance himself from the grittier aspects of his mob's operations, everything he did was colored by

his own criminality. He now controlled an ever expanding underworld organization that was gaining in influence and income every day: the 1920s were fertile ground for planting the seeds of vice, and Lucania knew how to make them grow.

In addition, his lieutenants often had their own empires, which they controlled themselves, so that Lucania's mob was essentially a criminal corporation, operating on a set of principles that were an aping of proper business practice. Lucania even demanded that his men dress with style and taste, be circumspect in their dealings and never, ever, break traffic rules when driving an automobile—you could never tell what a traffic officer might find in a gang member's car.

Lucania gave his lieutenants orders to 'organize' the neighborhoods of Manhattan for a colossal bookmaking operation: if you didn't make book for Lucania, your store, or ice cream cart, or fruit stand closed up due to the demise of its owner. Vito Genovese added a twist that enraged Lucania—he included junk peddling with the bookmaking operation: he was 'muscling' small merchants into selling heroin! Lucania deemed it an implausible risk, and put a stop to it.

The bookmaking operation grossed $500,000 per week. Lucania and Lansky also operated 'horse parlors,' where those who hadn't the inclination to go to the track could place bets and have the results brought in to them as soon as the race was over. These were comfortably furnished, with the best Scotch being served, and betting windows that simulated those that were used at the track. Ladies of polite

Above right: **Vito Genovese forced cart vendors to peddle his drugs as well as their wares. Country clubs similar to this *(below right)*, at Lake Placid, welcomed Lucania *(below)* for his booze.**

society were also welcome, and in general, the upper-class clientele of these parlors helped to make Lucania's 'outfit' so rich that he once proposed to a stockbroker that they sell shares in Lucania's operations on the open market!

Between the operations of Lucania, Lansky, Costello, Siegel and Adonis, the 'outfit' had a payroll of perhaps 100 men who plied various underworld trades. In 1925, Lucania collected receipts of $12 million on his alcohol sales alone.   Of course, the mobsters all claimed to have 'front' occupations upon which they paid taxes, but the real money was never properly taxed—which was to cause problems, notably for Al Capone in Chicago, among others.

At about this time, Meyer Lansky devised a way of claiming even the pennies that the very poor had in their possession: the numbers racket, whereby, with astronomical odds and a supposedly 'unriggable' winning number, ghetto dwellers could hope to win a huge sum by betting pocket change. This racket was officially named 'policy,' and it made the mob millions, and soon caught on with other 'outfits' all across the country.

Loan sharking was another 'angle' that had long been played by mobs. Italian immigrants were offered loans, only to discover that the rates were so high that they were forever in debt to the mobs, and existed as indentured servants. Lucania took it one step farther: by infiltrating the garment district through his lieutenants Charlie Lepke and Tommy 'Three Finger Brown' Lucchese, they offered the manufacturers similar loans to help them during lean periods in the ever-precarious climate of the fashion business. To complete their control, they conversely offered the garment workers unions monetary 'help' (with similar terms of payment) for their membership drives. Soon, the mob controlled the garment district.

When the manufacturer or the union representative couldn't pay up, he found himself with an 'overseer' from the mob, who would then bleed the business of everything it was worth; or would bleed the union for its workers' dues, and use the union as yet another machine for the promulgation of mob influence by offering or withholding the union's support come election time. The mob thus had sunk its fangs into legitimate business as well.

As of 1925, the Lucania mob decided to cash in on connections they'd been developing with the New York City Police Commissioner's Office. A payola arrangement was worked out: it began at $10,000 per week, and this rose—

during the tenures of commissioners Joseph A Warren and Grover A Whalen—to $20,000 per week.

Thus, the 'big fix' was in, and Lucania would have virtually unlimited mobility in New York City—it allowed him and his associate thugs to get away with anything they cared to inflict upon the public, and was yet another leg up toward gangland domination for them. Also, Johnny Torrio, on his way through town after an attempt on his life and a brief stint in jail in Chicago, met with Lucania and told him of his belief that Prohibition would end one day. Torrio proposed that Lucania start buying options on the best foreign Scotch in preparation for that day, which Lucania did.

It was at about this same time that Lucania and his men moved into influence buying at the state political level. They dealt with all comers, Republican or Democrat, whoever would serve the mob's purposes. Lucania now had control of Manhattan, which included Tammany Hall and the huge voting block that it controlled. Thus, the mob essentially made the careers of a number of state legislators.

Still, there were other considerations—the old Mafia bosses, for instance. In 1927, Masseria sent for Lucania. This time, based on his earlier considerations about Maranzano, Lucania went for the deal, on the condition that his whiskey business still remain his own concern, with no sharing, and that he would be second to no one but Masseria. Masseria agreed, and with that, Lucania was closer than ever to being the king of thieves that he had so long sought to be.

With beer from Schultz and his own whiskey, Lucania was soon supplying all of Masseria's speakeasies, as well as partaking of the massive loan sharking and protection rackets the old man ran.

Lucania modernized the Masseria empire, and new respect was granted him from gangsters all over the country—especially Capone in Chicago, who was having bloody battles with Bugs Moran and his gang, and felt it expedient to have a strong ally in the east. Then came the return from Italy to New York of Johnny Torrio, who was forced to flee Italy, and Benito Mussolini's anti-mob army. Torrio again came up with a spark of criminal genius: why not effect a merger with other major Eastern Seaboard bootleggers? It would offer increased strength, and would ensure a steady supply to all concerned.

They settled on, and achieved, a consolidation of seven of the strongest operations: Lansky and Siegel, who functioned as prime enforcers, protectors and shippers in New York and

New Jersey; Joe Adonis, with his Brooklyn empire; Longie Zwillman and Willie Moretti, who operated in western Long Island and northern New Jersey; Bitzi Bitz, Waxey Gordon and Nig Rosen in Philadelphia; 'King' Solomon, who ruled Boston and most of New England; Nucky Johnson who ran the South Jersey coast; and Lucania and Torrio.

They called themselves 'the Seven Group,' and by 1928, they had struck cooperative alliances with 22 different mobs in an empire that stretched from Maine to Florida, and from the Atlantic coastline to the Mississippi River.

In addition, Lucania was running a gambling business on the side with Arnold Rothstein and his associate, Frank Ericson. Besides running no-limit poker games, and with Ericson, managing a lucrative, high volume bookmaking operation featuring clientele in big business and the movie industry, Rothstein had also begun to move into the narcotics trade in a major way. Ericson, meanwhile, handled the duo's horse betting business.

Rothstein was shot to death on 4 November 1928, in a dispute over nonpayment of a gambling debt, at the Central Park Hotel in Manhattan. The gang took over Rothstein's end of the operation, and Ericson went on to become New York's most notable bookie for the next decade and a half.

Again, hijacking was cutting heavily into the whiskey business, and with bigger contracts than ever to fill, thanks to lucrative contracts with other 'Seven Group' members, Lucania was forced to scramble. He contacted a friend of Rothstein's named Samuel Bloom, who had supplied Capone with grain alcohol for years. Bloom came to visit and dropped in on one of Rothstein's games while he was on his way to Lucania.

Bloom lost all his money, but made the acquaintance of a fellow player who was the very man who owned the Scottish distillery that made King's Ransom Scotch Whiskey. Because of its heavy flavor, King's Ransom was a favorite among bootleggers, who found such pungent taste useful to their diluting operations.

He introduced the distiller to Lucania, and a deal was struck. Regular shipments of King's Ransom Scotch poured in through Nucky Johnson's South Jersey beachhead, and through King Solomon's Port of Boston. Bloom unfortunately arranged for his own 'cement overshoes' when he had a shipment hijacked to repay his gambling debts

Below: **A brewery raid.** *Below opposite:* **International Metal Polishers Union members—unions were targeted by the mob.**

1928. Bugsy Siegel 'sank' him in one of the rivers in the Manhattan area.

With their Tammany Hall clout, the gang was in demand come election time. Lucania, et al were contacted by Democratic New York State Governor Al Smith—he wanted, and received, their help in garnering the Democratic presidential nomination. Helped by the mob's influence in New York state, Smith swept the convention, only to be buried in the presidential election by his Republican opponent, Herbert Hoover.

Meanwhile, the competition between Maranzano and Masseria had broken out into war. The old Mafia Dons' hatred concentrated along the lines of their towns of origin: Maranzano was from Castellamare, so Masseria proclaimed death for any of Maranzano's Castellamarese troops: thus began the 'Castellamarese War.'

Masseria's demands on Lucania immediately grew more intense, and reached a peak when he insisted that Lucania participate in a payroll robbery, the kind of direct action that, since he had become a boss, Lucania was loath to do. The robbery went badly, and the robbers were apprehended with the money in their possession. Due to the fact that the mob had 'bought' the police commissioner, they were released, the charge declared an 'error.'

He had given the police an alias, Charlie 'Luciano.' Several times thereafter, he was hailed on the street by the new name. His own name, 'Lucania,' was hard for many people to pronounce correctly, so, in his second major name change, 'Charlie Lucania' became 'Charlie Luciano.'

After being freed following the arrest, he vented harsh words on Masseria, and the older gangster's pressure on him eased up. Lucania/Luciano then got on with the business of his 'bootleggers' conference,' an event that Masseria was not invited to. This meeting of the mobs was staged in the midst of Nucky Johnson's kingdom, at Atlantic City, New Jersey. Also, it held in conjunction with Meyer Lansky's honeymoon: he had paradoxically married a devoutly religious Jewish girl named Anna Citron in May of 1929. Her father was a big name in the produce business, a coincidence that would open doors for using her father's legitimate business for Lansky's illegitimate enterprises later on.

The purpose of the conference was to discuss a means nationwide underworld cooperation, which would decrease costly competitiveness, and would mean smoother operations for all concerned. This was accomplished. Also, the institution of wire service betting was given its beginnings, tying the national wire service to *The Daily Racing Form* via Moses Annenberg's connections with the Hearst news-

paper chain. Frank Ericson's track-betting expertise was the basis on which it was systematized.

Arrangements were also made to acquire shareholdings in legitimate foreign distillers in the event of the end of Prohibition. Also, the open gang warfare in Chicago had brought a lot of pressure to bear on gangs throughout the country. By way of placating the public with a false sacrifice, Al Capone was persuaded to 'take a fall' to friendly police for a minor weapons charge in Philadelphia.

Luciano emerged from this 'conference' as the leader of the most powerful underworld clique in the nation. He was, very shortly, to be the absolute leader of 'Gangland, USA.' He had an expensive suite in the penthouse of the Barbizon Plaza Hotel—a fact that made famous crime fighting reporter Walter Winchell furious, as he lived in the St Moritz, just across the street, and he loathed Luciano for the amoral, ruthless thug that he was.

Luciano's troubles with Masseria were not over. He was Masseria's criminal mastermind, providing for his lieutenants the same planning services that he had provided for Joe Adonis, whose penchant for theft—especially of jewelry—was a source of much wealth. Trouble with Maranzano heating up, Masseria demanded Luciano's time more and more, finally swearing that he was going to swallow not only Luciano's time, but his whiskey business, too. That was going too far. Yet, powerful as he was, Luciano's personal 'army' numbered perhaps 100 well-armed men. Masseria had over 500. Luciano contacted Maranzano, hoping to forge an alliance with which to 'rub out' his current 'boss.'

The meeting was arranged for a venue on Staten Island, a neutral territory run by Joe Profaci, and Luciano was to come alone, against the advice of Vito Genovese. Maranzano did not come alone, as per the agreement, but had several henchmen hidden in the shadows of the warehouse where they met.

When Maranzano revealed his stipulation that Luciano kill Masseria personally, Luciano refused on the grounds that, in the Sicilian code, by personally killing a boss, he would forever remove himself from ever becoming a boss. Upon that, Maranzano's men jumped Luciano, and torturing him for hours with belts and burning cigarette butts, tried to get him to capitulate. They later dumped him, unconscious but alive on a Staten Island street, where the police found him and took him to a hospital. Approximately 56 stitches were required to close his wounds. He would bear the facial stigma of a drooping right eye—caused by damage to a facial muscle sustained that night—to his grave.

Henceforth, Charles Luciano would bear yet another new name—due to the fact that he was one of few known gangsters to have ever 'gone for ride' and returned alive, he would now be known as 'Lucky': 'Lucky Luciano.' Soon came the stock market crash that ushered in the Great Depression. Suddenly, liquor sales were down, stolen goods fencing was down and slot machine earnings were down. One thing that kept going steady was the penny-ante numbers racket that Lansky had conceived, and it became the backbone of their operations.

The gang went into usury. Banks were extremely chary about loaning money in the depressed economy, the gangs

became the big, usurious, moneylenders for many citizens. Also, the nationwide wire betting service that Moses Annenberg had set up was now flourishing, and its profits poured into the mob's tills as well.

Luciano, never one to emulate the working people, or 'crumbs' as he called them, was now sure that he would never be one of them. Still, a few vestiges of normal life remained in him. In fact, he professed that once, on a Christmas visit to his family, '...for a few fast hours I almost wished I had a nine-to-five job....' Had he in fact, somehow, miraculously gotten a straight job, perhaps his criminal empire would not have gone on to flourish as it did, and millions fewer lives might have gone untouched by the virulent darkness of the underworld.

Day by day, the situation with Masseria and Maranzano was gaining in complexity, and was threatening to expand into wholesale bloodshed. Not only that, but a pivotal figure, Tom Reina, was threatening to leave Masseria, and side with Maranzano. Reina was Masseria's man in the Garment District. Luciano henchmen Lepke and Lucchese were just becoming entrenched with their loan sharking operations there, and they had just acquired an able 'enforcer,' or assault artist, named Abe Reles. Reina was on the brink of handing them the entire Masseria Garment District operation.

If Reina left Masseria, he would take Lucchese and his Garment District connections with him, thereby vastly complicating Luciano's Garment District operations. Luciano at first planned to talk Reina out of making his move too soon; but, in January, 1930, Masseria, enraged, informed Luciano of his desire to have Reina killed, as he had discovered Reina's intended treason.

Luciano had to move fast—and without trusted associate Meyer Lansky, who was preoccupied an extremely difficult domestic situation. Anna Lansky had given birth to a crippled child, and, never having approved of Meyer's criminality, poured forth a steady stream of vituperation. Sure that God had punished them for Lansky's sinful life, she had a nervous breakdown. It was more than Lansky, the professional thug, could handle. He fled New York in the escort of mobster Vincent 'Jimmy Blue Eyes' Alo.

Tom Reina met with Luciano, and having been told of the plans for his own death, exposed Masseria's plot to kill Joe Profaci and Joseph 'Joe Bananas' Bonnano—both, like Maranzano, Castellamarese. It became apparent that Masseria was trying to set Luciano up, and would try to make it appear

The Great Depression produced many unemployed (*at left*)—some spent their last dime in Lansky's numbers racket. *At right:* Battery Park, near the mob-infiltrated Garment District.

to Maranzano that, once the 'hits' were made, Luciano had engineered them, including the one on Reina. Maranzano would then expend his massive firepower on Luciano, and Masseria would claim all of Luciano's men and territory — the better to turn them, minus Luciano, against Maranzano.

Luciano determined then that Masseria would have to be killed before Maranzano, not *vice versa* as he and his gang had contemplated. Reina secretly made his switch to Maranzano, and Luciano contacted Albert Anastasia, and contracted for Masseria's death with him. Luciano then arranged for Vito Genovese to kill Reina, and to spread the word that Masseria had ordered the 'hit.' Genovese slew Reina with a shotgun on 26 February 1930, in front of Reina's favorite aunt's house, in the Bronx.

Masseria fell into the trap, greedily snatching up all of Reina's interests, and thus ruining what support he could have had from Reina's lieutenants. As for Luciano, the hit was done so that he could continue his own upward rise — it was a mere stepping stone. Masseria installed his lieutenant Joe Pinzolo in Reina's place, over Reina's lieutenants Gaetano 'Tom' Gagliano, Tommy Lucchese and Dominic 'the Gap' Petrilli, who swiftly plotted Pinzolo's demise.

Pinzolo was shot as he turned to face his killer, Dominic Petrilli, in Lucchese's office near Times Square. Before killing Masseria, Luciano's men had to eliminate Masseria's ace bodyguard, Pietro 'the Clutching Hand' Morello. Albert Anastasia and Frank Scalese killed Morello and a 'collector' named Pariano in Morello's loan sharking office.

Spreading rumors that the assassin had been an import from Chicago, Luciano's men convinced Masseria that Maranzano's Chicago ally, Joseph Aiello, had been responsible for the deed. Masseria dispatched favorite killer Al Mineo to Chicago, where he machine gunned Aiello to death on a street corner. In engineering the killing of Aiello, Luciano also fortified his alliance with Capone: Aiello had long been a costly enemy for Capone.

On 5 November 1930, Maranzano henchmen ambushed 'Joe the Boss' from a machine gun nest in an apartment that overlooked a known Masseria Gang meeting place. Masseria, Mineo and Steven Ferrigno were caught in the ambush. Mineo and Ferrigno were cut to ribbons in the hail of lead, but Masseria, ironically, escaped unscathed.

It was full scale war, and gangsters on both sides were gunning for each other on sight. Luciano and his men knew that this was a grand opportunity to catch Maranzano in their trap, just as they now had Masseria — even if he didn't know it yet. With the two Mafia Dons eliminated, Luciano would be on top.

Luciano, Lucchese, Joe Adonis and Bugsy Siegel met with Maranzano, Profaci and Bonnano at the Bronx Zoo, near the lion's cage. They discussed the killing of Masseria — who would do it, and what sort of protection Luciano and his men would get from Maranzano and his organization once the job was done.

An agreement was struck, and on 15 April 1931, Luciano talked Masseria into having lunch with him at the Nuovo Villa Tamaro restaurant on Coney Island — an offer that Masseria, an inveterate glutton, had not the willpower to refuse. Not only that, it was to be a celebration of Luciano's newly outlined plans for the wholesale slaughter of Maranzano's lieutenants: the plan itself was a ruse by which to manipulate Masseria.

After a long meal during which Luciano ate little — always being a sparing eater — and Masseria ate vast quantities of food, Luciano suggested a game of Klob, a Russian-Hungarian card game for two players that was popular in Manhattan at that time. The restaurant's owner, friend of many gangsters, Gerardo Scarpato, brought a deck of cards to the table and then 'went for a walk on the beach.' At the beginning of the second hand in the game, Luciano excused himself for a visit to the men's room.

As soon as he stepped into that facility, Anastasia, Adonis, Genovese and Siegel burst through the front door of the restaurant and started blasting at Masseria with their revolvers. They left as soon as they'd killed him, and Luciano re-entered the dining room, called the police, and of course, with no other witnesses present, said he didn't know who'd done it — he'd been in the lavatory.

Maranzano then installed himself as the 'Boss of Bosses' in a lavish ceremony that was attended by gangsters from all over the country, each of who bore a cash gift to show their fealty. At the end of the ceremony, Maranzano had collected a million dollars in such gifts, Luciano putting in $50,000 himself. Luciano was now, in addition to his own expanding operations, the second in command of the most powerful Mafia gang in America. Further, the machinery for the elimination of Maranzano was being put in place.

In preparation, Luciano, Lansky and gunman Mike Miranda surreptitiously visited gang leaders across the country, probing for support. Many of them felt that their positions would be enhanced if Luciano — less hidebound by Sicilian Mafia law, and altogether more dynamic than Maranzano — were to take the lead. Luciano and his allies set in motion a plan whereby the murder of Maranzano would be effected, and, upon its accomplishment, all of Maranzano's chief allies throughout the country would also be murdered. That would clear the way for the 'crowning' of Lucky Luciano as the chief of organized crime — both Mafia and non-Mafia — in the United States.

Maranzano had reason to believe he could trust Luciano. He was under the impression that Luciano had personally shot Masseria and therefore could not hope to be acceptable as 'Boss.' So, Luciano would have to be happy as second in line — all he could ever hope to be. One evening, in the heat of an argument, Luciano let slip the truth: he had not personally killed Masseria.

Maranzano, knowing what this portended, panicked. Very shortly, he set up a 'hit list' on Luciano and his closest allies. In order to preserve his own sense of gangland ethics — 'no one should ever harm another member of his own gang' — Maranzano hired a young killer named Vincent 'Mad Dog' Coll to carry out the killings.

Luciano and Lansky had, at the same time, decided that the perfect place and time to have Maranzano killed would be at his office in the Grand Central Building on Park Avenue and 46th Street, where Maranzano conducted his 'legitimate' front businesses — real estate and import -export brokerage. Knowing that Maranzano was more than eager to prove himself a legitimate taxpayer, and would readily open his cover-up books for any federal tax agents, Luciano and Lansky were sure that they had found a crack in Maranzano's usually unbreachable wall of protection.

They hired three anonymous-looking and little-known gunmen from Baltimore, Philadelphia and Boston, and named Red Levine, a trusted associate, to head the assassination team. They sequestered the men in a house on the outskirts of the Bronx, and tutored them on the proper demeanor, speech and carriage of federal tax agents.

In mid-1931, word came by way of Philadelphia that a Maranzano thug named Angie Caruso had told the tale of Maranzano's murder list during a drunken spree at an establishment owned by Nig Rosen. Maranzano's plan was formulated such that he would call Luciano and one of the other intended victims to come to his office for a meeting, but of course the only meeting would be of the victims and their intended killer.

Now knowing of his plan, Luciano and Lansky elected to dispatch Tommy Lucchese to the office when the call came, calculating that he would get there before Coll, would neutralize him with his own air of menace, and would generally try to set up the scenario whereby the 'tax agents' would pay their visit to Maranzano.

When Maranzano made the call, he was in the company of his secretary and five bodyguards. Coll had not yet come when Lucchese burst through the door, demanding to see Maranzano on urgent business. This served to throw Maranzano off balance and, suddenly, four 'federal tax men' burst in on the group, demanding that Salvatore Maranzano identify himself. He did, and, with a confirming gesture from Lucchese, the hit was on. They locked the door to the outer office, disarmed the bodyguards and hustled the still-unsuspecting Maranzano into his private office. Two stayed on guard with the secretary and the bodyguards, and two,

Aftermaths of violence analogous to Luciano's wars: Police and dead gangsters *(at right)*, and *(below)* bullet-riddled car.

slamming shut the inner office door, stabbed and shot Maranzano to death.

The murder accomplished, everyone, including the bodyguards, fled the scene of yet another crime to which there was later found to be 'no witnesses.' 'Mad Dog' Coll arrived too late, and, with $25,000 in his pocket for assignments he no longer had to perform, also fled the scene.

Luciano later claimed that it was then decided that the planned additional killings of Mafia 'old boys' across the US—did not have to take place. This was ostensibly conveyed in the calls that Luciano and associates made to all points in 'Gangland USA,' confirming that Maranzano was dead. Other sources, however, say that approximately 40 mobsters of 'the old guard' were slain across the country that day. In any event, the slayings were to be remembered as a phantasmagorically bloody evening, and were given an immediate and lasting infamy as the 'Night of the Sicilian Vespers.'

Whatever the carnage with which the media credited that day in gangland, there was one other documented murder that took place. Whether Luciano and his men, or someone else, saw a gangsterish 'necessity' in the act, it may never be known. At any rate, Gerardo Scarpato—owner of the Nuovo Villa Tamaro restaurant where Giuseppe Masseria was killed—was himself murdered that evening.

Maranzano was given the classic gangster funeral, complete with enormous mountains of flowers, many tears and flowery eulogies—Luciano insisted on that. He also insisted, as the new 'Boss of Bosses,' that a new age in crime was dawning.

Sensing that he could not control his associates through fear and intimidation as had Masseria and Maranzano—such tactics had resulted in both men's violent deaths—Luciano insisted on doing away with the 'coronation' *per se*. His 'crowning' was to be more of a convocation, at which he laid down the ground rules for not so much an empire as an underground corporation, with clearly defined areas of operation, and mutual cooperation for the profit of the whole. Also, Luciano insisted that an appeals process be set up for the underlings, or 'soldiers' of the mob, so that they could challenge decisions made by their superiors if the serious need arose.

Hence, 'The Syndicate'—organized crime as it is now known—was born. The meeting was held in Chicago, and Al Capone, though facing charges of income tax evasion, hosted the event like a gigantic party. For the first time at such an affair, the guest list for the premier event in gangdom was open to Jews, Irish and WASPs—not strictly Sicilians, as in the old days. Capone took over the Congress Hotel and part of the Blackstone: floors were assigned by city, and leaders were given the very best suites. The hotels were surrounded by Capone gangsters and hirelings from the Chicago police force.

The first afternoon, Luciano met with the leaders of various gangs, and gave them his *spiel*: each local and regional group would have considerable autonomy, but its leaders would each have a seat on a national board that would outline a national policy. This national policy would tie the organizations together. Luciano, as chairman by majority vote of his peers, would have one vote just like every other member of the board.

This was too much for some of the Sicilians: where was the 'Boss of Bosses' if Luciano didn't take on the role? Meyer Lansky advised Luciano to appease the Sicilians by naming the organization after something old and familiar—as if they were suffering from a 1930s underworld form of 'future shock.' Lansky's suggested name, which Luciano took up only for political reasons, to keep the Sicilians cool, was the 'Unione Siciliane,' the older organization of that name having by then taken on the Americanized monicker of 'The Italo-American Union.'

Despite his 'democratic' stance, Luciano was the de facto 'Boss of Bosses.' He was able to get what he wanted done, from coast to coast, and he was absolutely undisputed on his home turf—he owned underworld Manhattan. He could not, however, achieve *some* things. When Walter Winchell heard that Luciano was planning to move into the posh penthouse atop the St Moritz hotel where he himself lived, Winchell told the management that if Luciano moved in, he would move out, and further, he would publicize the reason for his moving out in his daily column in the *Daily Mirror*, and would label the St Moritz as a 'gangster hangout.' The St Moritz turned Luciano away.

He found another suite at the Waldorf Towers, where he paid the desk clerk to keep an eye on incoming traffic for him. He was registered as 'Mr Charles Ross.' His influence seemed to be capable of expanding beyond the usual circles when, in 1932, a presidential race was shaping up that could give the mob, or 'the outfit,' as Luciano liked to call it, tremendous leverage in national politics.

The Republicans were sure to nominate incumbent Herbert Hoover, who was assured of defeat due to his poor handling of the financial crisis that had afflicted the country

since the Wall Street Crash of 1929. The Democrats had a choice of Al Smith, already heavily indebted to the mob for favors supplied in past elections, and Franklin Delano Roosevelt, who was an unknown quantity in underworld terms.

In order to get a big vote in New York, a candidate was wise to court the substantial voting bloc represented by Manhattan—which meant courting Tammany Hall, which was controlled by the mob. In fact, corruption in Manhattan had become so bad that Judge Samuel Seabury was appointed to investigate it, and he was making things uncomfortable for Luciano and his cohorts. As a result of Seabury's investigations, the newspapers were rife with accounts of corruption in the New York City Police Department, courts and political circles.

Even so, the mob's Tammany Hall political machine was still in operation, even though Seabury was creating intense pressure on it: Lepke, Scalese, Vito Genovese and Luciano pooled an offer of two million dollars cash to 'buy' Seabury, and he immediately exposed the offer, trumpeting it through the newspapers in headline type. The gangsters became even more desperate. It became apparent that, since Roosevelt seemed to have the mark of a winner, that he would be the man to make a deal with in terms of getting Judge Seabury off the mob's back.

They reasoned that Roosevelt, being the governor of New York, would need their Tammany voting bloc to carry the state—if a man can't carry his own state, he could expect to lose his party's presidential nomination. For a favor, he could therefore be nominated as the Democratic candidate.

It certainly looked like 'the fix was in,' when an important

lawyer working for the Roosevelt campaign approached the hoodlums. An apparent deal was struck and—when Roosevelt made the announcement that he could not, at that time, continue to authorize Judge Seabury's findings—Luciano and 'fixing' associates Meyer Lansky and Frank Costello went to the Chicago Democratic Convention in the company of their 'marks,' Tammany leaders Jimmy Hines and Albert Marinelli, keeping them under strict observation and control. They were ready to hustle for Roosevelt.

At the convention, whiskey was offered openly by Capone lieutenants, 'The Big Fellow' himself having been imprisoned for income tax evasion just six months earlier, on 4 May 1932. The loose booze served to 'lubricate' some already free-flowing channels of influence, and helped to open a few new ones—a notable example of this latter being Huey 'Kingfish' Long, the infamous 'wide open' governor of Louisiana. After Lansky had plied him with sufficient whiskey, they went for a meeting with Luciano, Frank Costello and Moe Dalitz (a mobster from Cleveland). Here, the groundwork was laid for opening the entire state of Louisiana, and especially New Orleans, to the mob's gambling operations.

'Dandy' Phil Kastel was chosen to run the operation: he'd been an associate of Arnold Rothstein, and later on had underworld associations with Lansky, Costello and Adonis.

The convention was clearly leaning toward Roosevelt, and the word was passed along via Frank Costello that

Luciano moved up to the Waldorf Towers (at far left) in 1931. Below: 'Uptown' when he was a boy—Madison Square, 1908.

Roosevelt would live up to his promise to quash the Seabury investigation entirely. Luciano and his men had the Tammany politicians cast their voting bloc behind Roosevelt.

All's fair in love and war: for the United States of America, and for Franklin Delano Roosevelt, it was war against the mobsters. Roosevelt proved to be more than a match for Luciano. He was an extremely wily politician, and more than that, possessed a strong sense of moral certainty. The nomination in the bag for him, he suddenly declared himself definitely on the side of law and order, and turned Seabury loose on the mob. In concert with New York State Senator Fiorello H La Guardia, he declared that public office was a scared trust, and armed Seabury with the power to subpoena any and all parties under investigation, and vowed that, during his remaining term as governor, he would give Seabury all possible assistance.

Seabury pressured one crooked politician after another. A shining moment occurred when, after several difficult hours of questioning, New York Mayor Jimmy Walker chose to flee the country rather than risk further exposure. Tammany Hall was smashed, and several of its chiefs received sentences in Sing Sing Correctional Institution. New York City was hungering for reform.

The federal tax men were also beginning to cleanse the nation of some of its most notorious gangsters. After Al Capone's imprisonment on tax evasion charges, the next most conspicuous racketeer in the US was Dutch Schultz, who had changed his name from 'Arthur Flegenheimer.' He had grown up in the Bronx, and his police record listed 17 arrests ranging from disorderly conduct to murder. He became the 'King of Beer' among other things during Prohibition, and his colorful name was popular with editorial departments, resulting in loads of adverse publicity. He controlled all alcohol in the Bronx, and ran a protection racket whereby restaurants were assured that necessary

supplies—foodstuffs, etc—would indeed be delivered when needed, for a handsome fee, of course.

Schultz was one of the biggest numbers operators in the country as well, muscling in on the operations of black 'policy' bankers like 'Big Joe' Ison, Henry Miro and Alexander Pompez. Schultz's numbers racket took in $35,000 per day, and with the help of his accounting wizard, Otto 'Abbadabba' Berman, took a bigger slice of the profits than his agreements with his henchmen stipulated, though none could never prove it.

Other activities demanded Schultz' attention as well. The same Vincent 'Mad Dog' Coll that Maranzano hired to kill Luciano and his allies had started a war with Schultz back in 1931. It was a rather one-sided affair, with Coll losing his brother to Schultz gunmen. Then Coll perpetrated an act that was to tar him with the 'Mad Dog' monicker.

On 28 July 1931, Coll attempted a drive-by machine gunning of Schultz's man Joey Roa, who was at that moment seated in a lounge chair in front of the Helmar Social Club at 208 East 107th Street. Children were playing on the sidewalk nearby, and a baby lay asleep in a stroller not far away. Coll fired indiscriminately, wounding four of the children, killing the baby and leaving the Schultz mobster unscathed.

This caused a tremendous public outcry—something that mobsters, in this time of increasing reform, sought to avoid. On 7 February 1932, Schultz gunmen machine gunned Vincent 'Mad Dog' Coll as he answered a 'set-up' call in a telephone booth that was located inside the London Chemist Drugstore, at 314 West 23rd Street.

Schultz was soon to face a far more formidable enemy—the federal government began an investigation of his tax records, and soon developed a case against him for income tax evasion. In 1933, the government indicted Schultz for failure to report income for the years 1929–31. If convicted, he would face payments and fines of over $190,000, and a

At left: Prosecutor Thomas Dewey went after Schultz, but when Charlie Workman shot Schultz at the Palace Chop House *(below)*, Dewey went for Luciano. *At right:* Dutch Schultz on his death bed.

sentence of up to 43 years in prison. Thomas Dewey was preparing the case for the government.

Dewey had won tax convictions against the notorious independent assassin John 'Legs Diamond' Nolan, and had similarly triumphed over Waxey Gordon. He was gaining a reputation as 'the Scourge of the Underworld.' Schultz, now a wanted man, evaded arrest mainly through paying off the police.

However, with the election in January 1934 of the morally strong and courageous Fiorello La Guardia as Mayor of New York City, Schultz' fugitive status had not long to last. With mandates given him by US Secretary of Treasury Henry Morgenthau, Director of the FBI J Edgar Hoover and the electorate of New York City, La Guardia ordered his new police commissioner, Lewis J Valentine, to go after Schultz in earnest.

Schultz went underground, with the help of Albert Anastasia and Lucky Luciano. The search for Schultz was intensified, and La Guardia took such steps as regularly rounding up known gang members, raiding slot machine parlors (and destroying the machines) and naming Lucky Luciano as 'a no-good bum,' and as the *real* Public Enemy Number One.

The gangsters realized that Schultz was causing trouble, and urged him to settle up. His lawyer offered the government $100,000 in payment of back taxes, and was refused. Schultz gave himself up, and, winning a change of venue to Syracuse, was caught in an attempt to buy the jury of his first trial. A retrial was declared and, with another change of venue to the village of Malone, Schultz succeeded in buying the jury.

Meanwhile, his trusted associates in the mob were dividing Schultz's empire amongst themselves, sure that Schultz was out of commission. When a verdict of 'not guilty' was returned, the judge was outraged, but Schultz was free. The mob quickly covered up their attempt to steal Schultz's 'territory.'

He returned to New York and was subjected to much-deserved harassment from the police force. Fleeing to New Jersey, he became aware that his underworld assets were in danger of seizure from rivals, and he blamed the situation on a mobster named Bo Weinberg. Schultz set a trap for Weinberg, to see if he would try to contact the other suspected member of the 'takeover' team, Abner 'Longie' Zwillman. When Weinberg came to call on Zwillman, Schultz himself murdered him.

Schultz was not to be let escape. The New York City Attorney was corrupt, and as a direct result of his obvious underworld complicity, Thomas Dewey was appointed Special Prosecutor for the city. Dewey, undaunted by Schultz' jury-rigging, picked up where La Guardia and Valentine left off. He went after Schultz with a thoroughness verging on vengeance. Dewey very shortly developed an ironclad case against Schultz that included an indictment of his restaurant-protection racket and a murder charge for the killing of Jules Modgilewsky, aka 'Jules the Commissar,' a former Schultz enforcer who tried to cheat his boss.

While Luciano and his men were not sure that Schultz would be 'pinned,' without managing to wriggle free once again, they were concerned that Schultz was planning to 'wriggle free' by having Dewey killed—a move that, were it to succeed, would surely bring a fatal 'heat' down upon them all.

It was decided to have Schultz killed. Lansky abstained from the decision, telling Luciano that the 'heat' on Schultz was the only thing that prevented a similar pressure being exerted on Luciano himself. But the mob went through with their plans. On the night of 23 October 1935, Schultz went to one of his favorite restaurants, the Palace Chop House and Tavern, in Newark, New Jersey. While accompanied by bodyguards Abe Landau and Bernard 'Lulu' Rosencranz, and numbers manipulator 'Abbadabba' Berman.

Charlie 'The Bug' Workman and a second killer burst in upon the group as they sat at table, killing all of them save Schultz in a fusillade of lead. Schultz had, moments before, gone to the men's room: noticing the door ajar, Workman strode through it and put an end to the notorious life of 'Dutch' Schultz. Workman was convicted of the murders six years later, and was released from prison in 1964.

Luciano was now the primary target of Dewey's attentions. This sudden reversal of gangsterish fortunes was at least in part the result of a change in the national mood. Prohibition had dragged to a close at the end of 1933, but the damage had already been done. During Prohibition, a new breed of gangsters were born, and they were lionized by a general populace who in any other era would have viewed them as pariahs. However, given that these thugs and hoodlums were the only source of alcoholic beverages, people from all strata of society revealed their dependence on alcohol, and applauded all efforts to supply 'booze.' This gave the gangsters profit, protection from the law and time to develop a nationwide organization that was self-perpetuating (and rooted as stubbornly as any parasitic vine).

Gambling was now very big with the mob, and its tentacles surfaced in secretive casinos in Palm Beach; Covington and Newport, Kentucky; Hot Springs, Arkansas; Dade and Broward counties in Florida; Nucky Johnson's territory all along the South Jersey Coast; New Orleans and New York City.

In 1933, Meyer Lansky convinced his associates that Cuba was an untapped treasure trove—just 90 miles from Miami; and small enough to buy the government, lock, stock and barrel. Fulgencio Batista, the Cuban dictator, had been a friend to the mob since early Prohibition, and Lansky had no trouble 'buying' gambling rights to the island for three million dollars per year.

Eventually, Lansky, Luciano and the mob moved in on other islands in the Caribbean chain with their gambling operations. They also moved into legitimate businesses, using their loan-sharking operations as a wedge to force defaults, whereupon the mob took over legitimate garment, meat packing, trucking and other businesses. Another mob associate, 'Socks' Lanza, controlled the high-volume Fulton Fish Market on Manhattan's waterfront.

What the mob couldn't get by extortion, they got by threats—they offered businesses a choice: they could destroy shipments of perishable goods, or they could see to it that the goods arrived on time. Luciano's gang had indeed become an octopus.

Frank Costello and Phil Kastel set up Alliance Distributors, an importation business for the Scotch distillery that had supplied them with so much whiskey during Prohibition. Luciano, Siegel and others had a controlling interest in Capitol Wines and Spirits, Inc., another importation business for alcoholic beverages.

Meyer Lansky broke his old alliance with Bugsy Siegel and went out on his own. Using his father-in-law's business for a front, Lansky formed the Molaska Corporation, ostensibly a company that converted dehydrated molasses into a sugar substitute. But Molaska's real purpose was the use of the molasses as a base for the manufacture of quantities of illegal alcohol. Even with the repeal of Prohibition, bootlegging could turn a profit, due to the price differential between untaxed, illegal booze, and highly-taxed, legal whiskey. Molaska's distilleries were covertly located in New Jersey and Ohio, and its product was for sale to both bootleggers and 'legitimate' bottlers of well-known brands.

Vito Genovese, meanwhile, was setting up an international narcotics ring—a business that Luciano swore he never had anything to do with (of course, like most gangsters, he was known to utterly replace the truth with any self-serving statement that came to mind). Luciano's story was that Genovese had always loved the idea of selling narcotics, and would stop at nothing to do it.

Since it was a risky enterprise, and the mob did not approve it, Genovese had to turn elsewhere for his financing. A small-time thug named Ferdinand 'The Shadow' Boccia set him up with a Brooklyn merchant who loved to gamble. At a highly fixed poker game, Genovese took $50,000 from the merchant, and then for another $100,000 sold him a preposterous device said to be capable of churning out $10 bills.

Boccia, for his services, was repaid with a bullet in his head, and the thugs hired to murder him were then pitted against each other, which resulted in a farcical spectacle in which the one, Willie Gallo, took the other, Ernest 'The Hawk' Rupolo, to court for attempted murder, and got him convicted to a 20-year term.

It was the beginning of the end for Lucky Luciano, however. Since the Schultz murder, Thomas Dewey had targeted him as the next criminal who had to be put away. While he was the 'King of the Underworld,' Luciano was about to discover that his knack for distancing himself from the seamier—and more easily busted—aspects of 'the outfit' he ran would not, in the end, save him from prosecution.

The aim of Dewey's investigation was, from the early stages, to tie Luciano to the vice syndicate. At first, every attempt to deal a blow to Luciano directly was frustrated. Luciano's was a criminal empire built layer upon layer, and every man questioned seemed to have another man just above him who was equally distant from Luciano. Then came a crack in this protective layering—it was a break supplied from an unlikely source: the very lowest rung of the criminal ladder.

Assistant District Attorney Eunice Carter had been assigned the seemingly futile task of prosecuting prostitution cases. In her attempts to carry out her duties, she noticed that the girls were usually bailed out by the same men, and were represented by lawyers from the same law firm, who invariably brought along an 'advisor,' a disbarred lawyer named Abe Karp, who was know to be close to the Luciano underworld.

Mrs Carter was soon sure that prostitution in New York City had become a part of Luciano's empire, and took her findings to Special Prosecutor Dewey. Dewey hired her away from the DA's office, and provided her with two sharp young assistants, as he felt that such investigation had possibilities.

Mrs Carter and her aides kept turning up the same names in each prostitution case: Ralph 'The Pimp' Liguori, known to be a Luciano gang associate; James Frederico; Meyer Berkman; Jesse Jacobs; Benny Spiller; Abe Wahrman; Tommy 'The Bull' Pennochio; and 'Little Davie' Betillo.

Betillo's name came up so often that he became a focal point of the investigative effort. Dewey felt that the trail was 'hot,' and saw to it that Mrs Carter's team was joined by jurists Frank Hogan, Harry Cole, Charles Grimes, Stanley Fuld and Charles D Breitel—some of whom went on to become distinguished jurists in their own right.

To establish a case against Luciano as the ultimate 'boss' of the vice ring, they had to prove that he gave the orders for the various operations of the prostitution racket. They felt that Betillo and his fellow whoremasters might be the men to tell them. On 1 February 1936, a citywide raid was pulled on all the brothels in Manhattan. Whores, madams and their masters Liguori, Pennochio and Betillo were arrested. In round-the-clock interrogations, Dewey's staff questioned the prostitutes about their pimps, probing constantly for the name 'Luciano.'

In addition, the investigative team spread the word of an option arrangement, available to those under questioning: jail for silence; freedom for witnessing against the mob. The prisons were also informed of this, in case old henchmen or enemies under lockup had tired of confinement, and desired to come forth with evidence against America's top gangster, Charles 'Lucky' Luciano.

There being no true honor among thieves, this tactic proved to be quite productive. In March of that year, detectives were dispatched to Luciano's Waldorf Towers penthouse, but 'Charlie Lucky' escaped them by minutes. Fleeing to Philadelphia for a change of clothes, he then headed for the protective atmosphere of Hot Springs, Arkansas—a spa that had been the vacation retreat of many a mobster since the early 1920s.

Luciano was now Dewey's 'Public Enemy Number One in New York,' and was named in several criminal indictments as the head of a prostitution and vice ring that included Wahrman, Pennochio and Betillo. The indictments were handed down by a blue-ribbon grand jury that had heard, and found convincing evidence in, Dewey's findings.

There was now a nationwide manhunt on for Luciano. He was found strolling arrogantly along the promenade in Hot Springs, and extradition proceedings began. It became apparent that it would take tremendous pressure to pull Luciano out of the corrupted political milieu of Hot Springs. Dewey began firing off angry messages to Arkansas Governor J Marion Futtrell and state Attorney General Carl E Bailey. In addition, Dewey severely castigated the Hot Springs judge who had set Luciano free on $5000 bail. Governor Futtrell, embarrassed at being portrayed as a friend to mobsters, ordered Charlie 'Lucky' Luciano held for extradition hearings.

Hot Springs was in no hurry to give Luciano up for extradition. Its gangland connections over the years had provided the town with the wherewithal to become a major national resort. Refusing to transfer Luciano to Little Rock for an extradition hearing with the governor, the Sheriff of Hot Springs was soon faced with a detachment of Arkansas Rangers who had orders to storm the jail and take Luciano by force if the sheriff still would not give him up.

The sheriff complied. Luciano's underworld allies then approached Attorney General Bailey with a $50,000 bribe if he would quash the extradition proceeding. Bailey went public with news of the offer, refusing it and destroying any chances Luciano might have had to beat extradition.

He was extradited to New York City, where he faced a possible sentence of 1950 years in prison, on 90 counts, among which were charges of being involved with compulsory prostitution. Luciano gathered his legal counsel, heading his defense team with Moses Polakoff, one of the most high-powered lawyers in New York. Luciano's biggest complaint was that he was being charged with being in the prostitution racket—an embarrassment to a gangster who hypocritically felt that prostitution was something to make money from, but never to be admitted as part of one's own doing, in the sick ethical system of gangland.

His bail was set at $350,000. Once the gang posted this, and rushed with their besieged chieftain to the Waldorf Towers penthouse, Polakoff informed Luciano, Lansky, Siegel, Costello, Adonis, Lucchese, Anastasia, Torrio and a few others gathered there, that the charges would be hard to

Opposite: A bathhouse at Hot Springs, Arkansas—once popular with Luciano's ilk. *Below left:* An April 1936 headline of his extradition. *Below:* A cartoon on the federal crackdown.

LUCIANO ON WAY TO NEW YORK IN SURPRISE MOVE

Lawyers Napping as Vice Lord Given to Officers.

German Army Fliers Fall in Switzerland

Biel, Switzerland, April 17 (Friday) (AP).—Two persons were killed and two others were missing early today as a German army plane fell in the Swiss mountains, 30 miles from the German frontier.

The plane carried five uniformed men. Authorities said the fifth occupant was an officer who suffered a broken leg and refused to give information about the flight.

Catching flat-footed the high-priced staff of lawyers hired by Charles Luciano, Attorney General Carl E Bailey and Prosecuting Attorney Fred Donham turned the accused king of New York racketeers over to New York detectives at 12:01 this (Friday) morning.

Custody of the prisoner was transferred at the county jail. Sheriff Branch made the formal transfer but he did so on authority of Mr. Bailey and Mr. Donham both of whom were at the jail.

Several State Rangers aided the New York officers in guarding Luciano as he left.

Luciano had elapsed, and the other his own status on the retired list. He said that a decision on the subject should be made by Judge Kimbrough Stone of Kansas City, presiding judge of the Circuit Court of Appeals, if made by anyone.

Judge Stone, who notified Panich last week that he would consider a petition for the right to appeal the Luciano case up to 2 p. m. last Monday, said at Kansas City last night that Panich conferred there yesterday with him and with Judge Arba S. Van Valkenburgh, retired judge of the court. He said that Panich told them he planned to file

beat: he was sure that Dewey had a solid case, and it would be no 'walkover.'

Albert Anastasia—who, together with Tommy Lepke, headed the mob's assassination squad (known to the press as 'Murder, Incorporated')—recommended that they simply kill Dewey. Anastasia had obliterated his conscience in the course of committing at least 63 murders. (He was arrested for four of these, but had no convictions—due to the fact that the witnesses mysteriously disappeared, never to be seen again.)

Luciano said 'That ain't the way…at least, not now.' Confident that Dewey could not possibly have tied him to the mob's vice ring, Luciano was sure that his sharp lawyers would 'make mincemeat' of the prosecution's witnesses, especially when he heard that most of the witnesses were low-class prostitutes—not even 'crumbs' in Luciano's scale of values, but those who he and his associates had forced into depths that the average 'crumb' could barely imagine.

The words 'compulsory prostitution' define a crime so loathsome that Luciano and his lieutenants—men who murdered others as a matter of convenience—were desperate to avoid being connected with it, even though they, in fact, had perpetrated and helped others perpetrate it many times over. Public outrage had become intense. Essentially, it involved white slavery, the machinations of which are described in the 'Al Capone and His Underworld' segment of this book.

Many of the girls had been kidnapped and brutalized in the gang's primitive form of 'brainwashing'; others were subsumed into it by their gangster boyfriends; still others were the victims of mob 'sponsors' who got them hooked on narcotics, and functioned as their 'pushers' until the girls were so deeply in debt for drugs that prostitution became an even darker part of the nightmare that they'd fallen into.

Luciano and his men had, in the authorizing and commission of such 'enterprises,' become the very filth of the gutter, corrupting and wasting the lives of countless young women. Their sole excuse was the enormous hypocrisy that the girls were 'nothin' but dirty whores.' They themselves were the true whores, having sold their souls long before.

Luciano and his nine co-defendants were tried on the compulsory prostitution charges, the first court date being the sunny morning of 13 May 1936. Justice Philip J McCook presided over the trail, which featured a carefully-selected panel of 12 straightlaced jurors who had proved invulnerable to the sort of corrupting influence that other gangster trial jurors of the period had so often knuckled under to.

Thomas Dewey made his opening remarks, indicating that prostitution had always been an operation run by 'independents,' until Luciano put out the word to these independents that he was taking over the racket, and would install Dave Betillo as his lieutenant in charge of the racket. The syndicate controlled more than 200 whorehouses in Manhattan, the Bronx, Queens and Brooklyn, and grossed over a million dollars per month.

Dewey went on to assert that at no point did Luciano directly collect money from the girls; the vice industry was too well organized for that—but, every move that Betillo made was dictated from the top, and the man at the top was none other than 'Lucky' Luciano.

Then began the testimony for the prosecution. Lasting three weeks, it involved 68 witnesses, most of whom were girls and madams, who implicated Ralph Liguori as the mob's procurer, and defendants Betillo, Pennochio, Berkman and Spiller as men they had seen frequently at the houses, but none of whom had been customers. Most of these girls were extremely faded individuals, apparently without a sense of hope left, and many of them drug addicts.

It was a spectacle calculated to tear the tough veneer off the most hardened cop, as girls who had come from all walks of life came to testify of the men who had brought them so low. They talked about the bail bonding service, about the stories that Abe Karp had coached them to tell to the magistrate's court, and about how they could not tell the truth when arrested, under pain of sure death at the hands of a mobster.

They spoke of the various ways the mob had of keeping them terrified and dependent on the vice ring. The repetition of story after story created an overwhelming sympathy for the girls on the part of judge and jury. The very mention of the mobsters' names increasingly evoked a tense negativity on the part of those present in the courtroom, and the mention of Luciano's name, even in passing, created a palpable hostility.

Then began a new phase in the prosecution: co-defendants who had pled guilty and were subpoenaed as witnesses took the stand. The first was a lowlifer named Al Weiner, whose 35 houses of prostitution had been taken over by Betillo under threat of death. After having been subjected to an unsuccessful drive-by shooting, Betillo had told him he'd better submit 'or Charlie would take care' of him.

While 'Charlie' was not properly identified, and while Luciano's lawyer George Morton Levy strenuously objected, and was sustained, the name 'Charlie' hung above Luciano like the Sword of Damocles. There was no elaboration or identification necessary. For years people had known that Luciano was the head of crime in New York, and this was simple corroboration.

A few days later, the 'sword' began to lower. Peter Balitzer, aka Peter Harris, had been operating one of the biggest cesspools of corruption in the city when Betillo approached him about takeover, offering to set him up as a syndicate manager and bookkeeper. Betillo prodded him, saying 'Don't worry, Charlie Lucky is behind it,' further adding that Balitzer should never mention Luciano's name to anyone, 'or else.'

Then, Balitzer testified, one of the houses were held up by young mobsters. These young thugs were rounded up by Abe Wahrman and associates, and were taken to a remote spot for a punitive beating. Abe Wahrman told them, 'Didn't I tell you to keep away from those houses because they belong to Charlie Lucky?'

Then came testimony from a convicted thug named Joe Bendix, who had interrupted his lifetime stay at Sing Sing to testify, having answered the call that Dewey had put out through the penal system.

Bendix had known Luciano since 1929, when he used to associate with him and other patrons of Ducore's Drug Store on Seventh Avenue. In 1935, after several terms in prison, he realized that if he were to practice his usual 'trade,' theft, he would receive a life sentence as a recidivous thief. He therefore turned to an acquaintance, Jimmy Frederico, and asked him about getting a job as a collector in the prostitution racket. At least, busted for that, he would have a few more busts left before life imprisonment once more became a threat.

Frederico took him to see Luciano, who was puzzled as to why his old acquaintance would want such a low-paying job when his thievery could make more money. Bendix explained himself, was 'interviewed' by Luciano again, and was offered a job. By that time, Bendix had reverted to stealing, and soon thereafter committed a theft for which he was caught and 'sent up for life' at Sing Sing.

Levy cross-examined Bendix, and established that he had, indeed, received promise of a reduction in sentence for his testimony. Even with that admission, Luciano was in deep trouble.

Then came a witness that was to blow Luciano's confidence completely. Her name was Florence Brown, aka 'Cokey Flo.' She had been a romantic interest of Frederico's when she was fifteen, and he enticed her into prostitution. She had been a drug addict since that time, too, and was now

Below: Albert Anastasia, who wanted to kill Thomas Dewey. *At left:* Luciano on trial—smug before Dewey started grilling him.

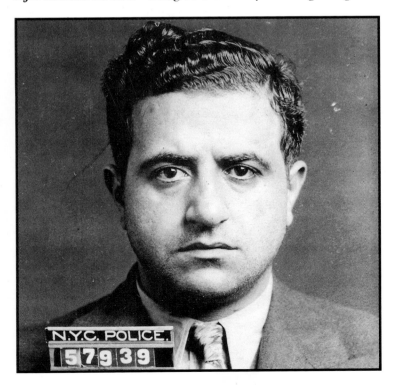

N.Y.C. POLICE
57939

in her mid 20s, even though at times she looked like a waif, and at others like an ancient crone who had the blood of youth leeched out of her.

She had been present when Luciano said 'We're gonna organize the cathouses like the A&P (an early supermarket chain).' He went on to say they could put the madams on commission, forcing more and more work out of the girls. She had also been present when he gave instructions for the torture and intimidation of girls and madams, so that they would work without complaint, round the clock. 'First you got to step on them. Talking won't do no good. You got to put the screws on,' he said.

Still more damaging could have been the testimony of Nancy Presser, who had been a prostitute and drug addict since the age of 13, and seemed to have had involvements with mobsters ranging from Waxey Gordon to Joe 'The Boss' Masseria, and, of course, Charlie Luciano. But when, upon cross-examination, she failed to properly describe places where she claimed to have been, her testimony was discounted.

Dewey had subpoenaed witnesses from among the staff of the Waldorf Towers and the Barbizon to show that Luciano had met with, and thus been involved with, his co-defendants for years, and thus had been involved in the running of the prostitution racket on a long-term basis.

In addition, Dewey made an announcement to the court that his witnesses were under constant danger from the mob's assassins. This announcement caused Justice McCook to warn the defendants that they would be held personally responsible if any of the prosecution's witnesses were harmed or intimidated in any way.

Then came testimony from Mildred Balitzer, a madam who helped her husband in strong-arming other women during the operation of their string of whorehouses. Betillo muscled in on them, saying he was working for 'Charlie Lucky.' Later, in the company of Betillo, she met Luciano in a restaurant: he was introduced to her as 'the boss.'

Dewey rested his case on 29 May 1936. Luciano attorneys Polakoff and Levy advised him not to testify, but he insisted. He took the stand on 3 June. After brief questioning from his own counsel, and making a statement that he had never 'gotten a single dollar from a prostitute or from the prostitution racket,' Prosecutor Dewey took over.

Dewey quickly established that Luciano had been involved in nothing but criminal activity for the previous 18 years, and hadn't had a single legitimate enterprise. He also quickly established, through direct questioning, that Luciano was a compulsive liar, and had at least five aliases.

Dewey closed in, asking him in rapid succession if he had ever known Lepke, Shapiro, Siegel, Masseria, Capone or Terranova. Luciano answered 'yes' to all but the last two. Dewey then retrieved from the prosecution table, and read off in a loud voice, Luciano's telephone records from the Waldorf Towers and the Barbizon Plaza. They were rife with calls from Luciano's phone to Ciro Terranova's unlisted number in Pelham, New York, and to Capone in Chicago. Luciano claimed it must have been someone else who broke into his apartment to make those calls.

And then came the 'clincher.' Dewey read off, from the same records, repeated calls from Luciano to the vice ring's headquarters—Celano's Restaurant, on Manhattan's Lower East Side. Luciano tried once more, as he had so many times in his misbegotten life, to wriggle free of this latest hook upon which he'd impaled himself. He blandly stated that Celano's spaghetti was good, and he liked to make reservations.

Despite his attempts to appear calm and collected, Luciano was sweating so that his clothes were soaked. Dewey kept it up, for hour after hour. At the end of the day, it was apparent to all that 'Charlie Lucky' was not so lucky after all: among other things, he was a scurrilous bum who, in concert with all mobsters of all times and places, had burrowed his way into society, attempting to bring it all down to the dank depths that he himself dwelled in.

He was at times a deceptively charming man, but his propensity for lying had become so much a part of him that he justified his every action with a lie. Again and again he would deny ever being involved 'in the prostitution racket,' but as the self-confessed overlord of the vast, rotten quagmire of American organized crime, he most certainly participated, and reaped the cash benefits from the ruined lives of his victims.

He himself also admitted that he had made his rise on the deaths of others, on double crosses and chicanery, and on activities that were one hundred percent based on bribery, intimidation and threat of murder. His associations and 'alliances' were all subject—as they were with every gangster—to the perceived necessities of the moment. A telling ritual of traditional gangs was that a 'hit' was only honorable if it was done face-to-face: therefore, the victim was likely to be turning in greeting to a known and trusted associate, rather than fleeing an unknown assassin.

As for the 'civilian' victims of the mob, they were killed without a thought to anything but the welfare of the mob. The old Sicilian Dons, often portrayed as 'Robin Hoods,' in truth took everything their poor countrymen had, and lived in opulence by draining the resources of the hardworking communities to which they had, like bloodsucking organisms, attached themselves.

It is a crashing irony that Luciano's own mother and father had to secret their hard earned money away from the view of their local Don for a decade before having enough to afford their passage to America. The Dons fancied themselves royalty. Whereas a true king leads and protects his people, the Dons and their American spawn, like Luciano, existed solely to victimize the people.

It was 5:25 am on 7 June 1936, and Charlie 'Lucky' Luciano, a man who instituted a new era of racketeering and ruthlessness in America, was found guilty of all counts for which he had been tried. Luciano received a total of 30–50 years in state prison, commuted in 1946 (for encouraging his 'outfit' to help with the anti-espionage war effort) to exile to his native Sicily, under extensive surveillance, and with a dusk-to-dawn curfew.

While he was, in part, able to run part of the mob's operations from prison, and then from exile, he was never again to so completely hold the reigns of power as he had before Thomas Dewey's investigations. In the late 1950s, it became apparent that Luciano had a bad heart. With this knowledge, and the pain of increasing angina pectoris attacks, 'Charlie Lucky' sought to retire from his mob activities, but the mob warned that he could only do so upon pain of death.

Lucky Luciano's last days were filled with anxiety: one of his old mob cohorts, Vito Genovese, had decided to set him up for a narcotics bust. Genovese sought to put his old boss away in classic style: he could not kill a 'boss' personally if he expected his underlings to respect him. Therefore, he sought to arrange a prison sentence for Luciano that would also effectively be a 'hit,' considering Luciano's seriously diseased heart.

The strain and frustration felt by Luciano upon becoming aware of this, and the increasing pressure on the part of the Italian Guardia (Italian National Police)—exacerbated by Genovese's efforts—produced the massive heart attack that killed Salvatore 'Charlie Lucky Luciano' Lucania on 25 January 1962.

Below left: 'Lucky' Luciano makes the headlines in *The Arkansas Gazette* of 8 June 1936. *Below:* Jean Bell, one of Luciano's vice ring victims, added to the stunning testimony that helped put 'Charlie Lucky' in prison. *At right:* Vito Genovese, heroin pusher, was Luciano's long-time nemesis, and applied the pressure that led to Luciano's death by heart attack on 25 January 1962.

ARKANSAS SHARES IN CREDIT FOR BREAKING LUCIANO VICE REIGN

Whatever it was that caused Charles Luciano to choose Arkansas as a haven, he probably would concede now that it was a mistake. Nicknamed "Lucky" after his miraculous return from a "ride" on which underworld rivals took him several years ago, he seemed to realize that his luck had run out when he was locked up in the Pulaski county jail.

That was on April 5, and for 10 days thereafter Luciano's lawyers sought desperately to block his return to New York. But at every turn they encountered Attorney General Carl E. Bailey, whose aid had been enlisted by Edward McLean, assistant racket prosecutor from New York.

Luciano, arrested April 1, had hoped to dodge an extradition hearing before Governor Futrell by remaining at Hot Springs, his headquarters during his stay in Arkansas. He was not averse even to staying in jail there, temporarily, and was taking steps to effect his

—Associated Press Photo.
CHARLES ("LUCKY") LUCIANO.

LUCIANO, EIGHT OTHERS GUILTY IN VICE COMBINE

Face Life Terms In Prison.

New York, June 7 (AP)—Charles Luciano, known to the underworld as "Lucky" since the time he came back alive from a gangland ride, was convicted on all 62 counts of a vice indictment by a jury early today.

Eight co-defendants, indicted with Luciano as overlords of a $12,000,000 compulsory prostitution syndicate in the

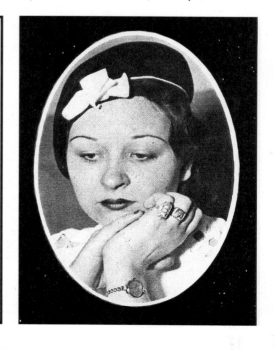

Infamous Rural and Suburban Outlaws

John Dillinger

John Dillinger was born in 1903, and was raised in Indianapolis, Indiana. He was a gifted athlete in school there. As a teenager, he and his family moved a few miles to the southwest and settled on a farm near Mooresville. He was an intensely proud boy, very emotional, and was often out of self-control. As a lark, when he was 20, he stole a car.

The thrill having worn off, he feared arrest and joined the Navy. That was not the end of his impulsiveness, and in his increasingly chaotic view of life, there was nothing wrong with deserting from the Navy, and so he did, just as he had stolen the car.

Again impulsively, he married a girl in Mooresville, and when this attempt to settle down was faced with the usual difficulties, Dillinger's underdeveloped personality failed to respond constructively. To disagreement, there was a response of anger; to material need, there was the response of immediate gratification: he and an acquaintance tried to rob a grocer in September, 1924 and were successfully repulsed.

The police picked them both up a short while later, and they received prison terms at Indiana City State Penitentiary. Dillinger's was unusually long—nine years—and in his time behind bars, he began to manifest the truly desperate state of his psyche. He attempted escape five times.

While incarcerated, he met the men who would form 'The John Dillinger Gang' when they were all released. These were Harry Pierpont, John Hamilton, Russell Clark and Charles Makley—all of them bitterly angry at the society that dared to punish them for their crimes. They literally felt that they were above everyone else, and as selfish, thwarted individuals, they felt that everyone else owed them a living.

Between escape attempts, Dillinger and his future gang decided upon their career of crime, and—like Bonnie Parker and Clyde Barrow and the Barker gang—were possessed of the warped vision of the bank robber and outlaw as hero. The gang developed plans for Dillinger—scheduled to be the first released of any of them—to commit a series of robberies, the proceeds from which would finance a massive jailbreak for the rest of them.

He was paroled in May, 1933, and soon gathered around himself a gang of desperadoes with whom he pulled a number of bank heists. With his share of the money from these robberies, Dillinger bought pistols and hid them in a shipment of thread that was destined for the shirt factory at Indiana City Penitentiary, where several of Dillinger's cronies were assigned to the work detail.

Dillinger's cronies succeeded in breaking out of Indiana City on 26 September 1933. That very day, Dillinger was arrested while visiting a girlfriend in Dayton, Ohio. Playing tit for tat, Dillinger's newly freed comrades, in cooperation with the rest of the gang, broke Dillinger out of jail on 12 October of that year. Pierpont, Makley, Clark, Hamilton and new member Edward Shouse entered the Lima, Ohio county jail, and demanded to see Dillinger 'for questioning.'

When the desk officer, Sheriff Jess Sarber, asked to see their credentials, they killed him and, using his keys, freed Dillinger. Not long after, Pierpont and Dillinger approached the desk at the Pierpont, Indiana police arsenal.

Disguised as interested tourists, they asked the policeman on duty what kind of defenses the police had in case 'the notorious Dillinger Gang' came to town. When the officer proudly unlocked a case of Thompson submachine guns to awe them with police firepower, Dillinger and Pierpont pulled their guns, and stole not only machine guns, but pistols, shotguns and bullet proof vests as well.

Specializing in bank robberies, the gang perpetrated a spree of daring, machine gun-waving daylight raids. Dillinger's psychotic flamboyance, and his seeming need to flout the law soon gained the gang spectacular notoriety.

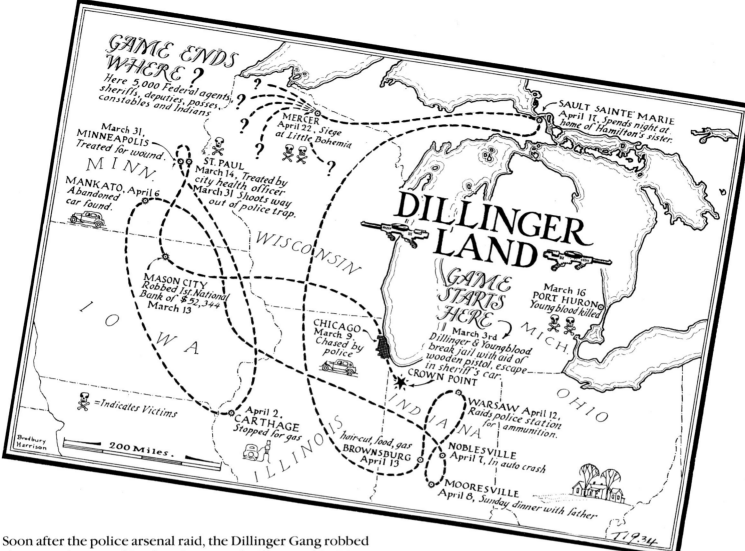

Soon after the police arsenal raid, the Dillinger Gang robbed the Central National Bank in Greencastle, Illinois of $75,000 in cash and bonds.

Several weeks after, Dillinger's growing notoriety resulted in a high speed auto chase by policemen through the streets of Chicago, cutting short a Dillinger visit to a doctor's office. Feeling that the Illinois/Indiana area was growing too 'hot,' the gang fled to Wisconsin, where they took hostages while robbing a bank in Racine. They let the hostages go free after successfully eluding police.

From Wisconsin, they went to Florida and hid there for a while. Needing money, and seeking a change of venue, they travelled northwest toward Arizona. It was alleged—and denied by the gang—that they stopped by Chicago and robbed the First National Bank, killing a police officer in their escape.

Dillinger's trademark flamboyance including wearing dapper clothes, smiling a great deal, and athletically leaping over countertops while holding the populace at bay during bank robberies. He and his gang made a point of saying 'please' and 'thank you,' and of holding doors open for ladies in the course of their crimes: they wanted to be known and, ironically, respected as gentlemen-outlaws.

They felt, like Lucky Luciano, that the world of working for a living was for 'crumbs.' It was, of course, a sign of their own weakness that they could not bear the light constraints of normal human behavior.

And then it seemed, on 25 January 1934, that John Dillinger and his gang had done their last illegal acts, when

Above: A graphic, from a 1930s magazine, tracing some of Dillinger's exploits—starting with his infamous Crown Point jailbreak on 3 March 1934. *Below:* A wanted poster for Dillinger.

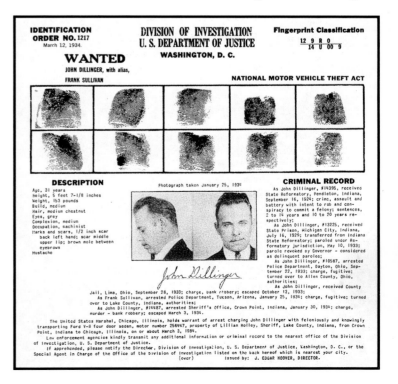

Tucson, Arizona police officers captured the Dillinger Gang without firing a shot.

Their hotel had caught on fire, and firemen carrying out valuables noted that one of the suitcases was extremely heavy. Opening it, they found it was crammed with weapons. Quietly, the police rounded up these gun-toting 'guests' one by one.

John Dillinger himself was transported to a new jail at Crown Point, Indiana, which was built to be 'escape-proof.' While its physical plant was no doubt secure, the frailty of human judgement allowed the killer to escape.

Dillinger somehow obtained a razor blade and a block of wood, and proceeded to carve a fake pistol. With the application of shoe polish, his 'gun' could, with the right amount of intimidation on Dillinger's part, be mistaken for the 'real thing.'

He held his jailers at bay on 3 March 1934, fake pistol in hand. He stole Sheriff Lillian Holley's car and fled across the state line into rural Illinois. Up to that point, he had in fact been a candidate for extradition to a number of states, but he had not been wanted by the FBI, as he had not yet broken a federal law. When he fled across the state line in a stolen car, however, the FBI very eagerly came in on the case, and Dillinger's days were numbered.

Dillinger, taking just a few days, assembled another gang of outlaws, the most notorious of them being Lester 'Baby Face Nelson' Gillis. Within a week after Dillinger's escape from Crown Point, the new gang robbed Security National Bank in Sioux Falls, South Dakota. The day before the robbery, a gang member came to town, spreading rumors of a movie filming that was to take place the next day. Therefore, while the robbery was in progress, the citizenry gawked at what they thought was a Hollywood production. The illusion ended when Baby Face Nelson killed a policeman.

Not long after, Dillinger and another gang member were wounded during a robbery in Mason City, Iowa. Dillinger then

At left: Dillinger, with the wooden pistol he wielded at Crown Point, and a submachine gun. *Below:* His gang's arsenal. *Below right:* Chicago's Biograph Theater, where he died on 22 July 1934.

ARSENAL OF DILLINGER AND GANG

repaired to the St Paul, Minnesota apartment of girlfriend Evelyn 'Billie' Frechette. The FBI, knowing that Dillinger had long since ceased any relationship with his wife, were aware of Billie Frechette's role in his life.

On 31 March 1934, FBI agents knocked at her door, and, stalling for time, she allowed Dillinger to gather his weapons before slamming the door and fleeing out a rear entrance with him. The situation was further complicated when a Dillinger henchman began climbing the front stairs, unaware of the federal agents. Momentarily lucky, Dillinger ran into more agents in the street, and was wounded in the gun battle that ensued.

Rendezvousing with his gang hours later, Dillinger convinced them that a 'vacation' was in order. The Dillinger Gang then retired, momentarily. Less than a month later, on 22 April, the 'Little Bohemia' resort hotel in rural Wisconsin was the scene of yet another pitched battle.

By this time, Special Agent Melvin Purvis was on the case. Purvis was a man with boundless enthusiasm for hunting outlaws. He acted on a tip and surrounded the Little Bohemia with dozens of FBI agents. It was a disaster for the FBI, in which two private citizens left the hotel, were told by the FBI to 'hold it,' but kept on walking.

The agents opened fire, killing one of the men and wounding the other. Then the gangsters, attempting to leave by a rear exit, were involved in a roaring gun battle with agents on that side of the hotel. Still, they escaped without injury, leaving their girlfriends to 'face the music.' Altogether, two bystanders and two FBI agents were wounded, and a bystander and an FBI agent were killed.

Ironically, the press was busy pumping Dillinger up, and comparing him with everyone from Tom Sawyer to Abraham Lincoln. As if that foolishness weren't enough, *Time* magazine came out with a Dillinger board game, tracing his exploits from the Crown Point escape onward. There is every evidence that all the publicity fed his pride, and

encouraged him to continue his life of robbery and killing.

The publicity also had another effect: FBI Director J Edgar Hoover increased the pressure to stop this thug who was 'making a mockery of the law.' US Attorney General Homer Cummings admonished police forces to 'shoot to kill.'

Dillinger was now Public Enemy Number One. The FBI offered a $10,000 reward, and the banks that Dillinger had robbed put up a matching $10,000 for his arrest and/or slaying.

Dillinger began to worry, and went to a Chicago underworld doctor, James J Probasco, for a bit of plastic surgery: he had his face lifted to appear younger, then dyed his hair and grew a moustache. Probasco, upon being questioned by FBI agents, leaped to his death from a nineteenth floor window.

Then, a notorious underworld figure named Anna Sage stepped forward to offer a deal. She was slated for deportation as an undesirable alien, but, if the FBI could promise that she could avoid deportation by doing so, she would set Dillinger up for them.

Thus it was that, on the evening of 22 July 1934, Melvin Purvis and a group of 'G-men' (a Hollywood gangsterism for FBI agents) blended into the crowd in front of Chicago's Biograph Theater. Purvis, acting as director of the operation, stationed himself in a car that was parked nearby.

Dillinger and Anna Sage (fictionalized in the newspapers as 'The Mysterious Lady in Red') were inside the Biograph, watching Manhattan Melodrama, a movie about boyhood pals in the slums of New York. One of them grew up to be a District Attorney, and the other became a mobster. The movie over, Dillinger and his treacherous 'date' left the theater.

Upon seeing Dillinger, Purvis lit a cigar to signal his fellow agents. Dillinger saw the agents coming for him, and drew his pistol, whereupon the agents shot him down. John Dillinger, determined to live his life entirely his own way, lay dead on a gritty Chicago street, at the age of 31.

Pretty Boy Floyd

'Pretty Boy' was the name Oklahomans gave this foppish, rowdy ex-farmboy who became notorious for terrorizing the countryside in the early 1930s. His favorite weapon was the Thompson submachine gun, and it was by this same instrument that he died. He gained a popular following by robbing unpopular banks in Depression-stricken eastern Oklahoma; his habit of freely spending the money helped to build a not-very-accurate reputation for him as a 'Robin Hood' figure of sorts. This brought him protection and fame, and was probably intended to do so.

Charles Arthur Floyd was born in Oklahoma in 1901. He grew up on a dirt farm there, and himself attempted to make a living as a farmer. Sometime during this period, he got married, and then an event happened that was to color his life from that point on: a man shot and killed Floyd's father. His wife pregnant, and the farm not doing well, the bitterness over his father festered inside him, and he himself took up a gun.

He abandoned even his wife for a life of crime, of revenge, as if no one had ever suffered as he had. In approximately 1927, he robbed a payroll in St Louis, was apprehended, and spent three years in prison. He swore that he would never spend time in prison again. Ironically, he was now completely imprisoned in his growing mania. Upon his release, he sought out and shot the man who had killed his father. That was not the end of it; violent crime had become his passion.

Now a hunted man, he fled to Kansas City. Using that municipality as a base, he robbed several small town banks in 1930. On one occasion, the driver of his getaway car smashed into a telephone pole, and Floyd was arrested, tried and convicted for armed robbery, receiving a sentence of 15 years in the penitentiary. On his way via train to prison, Floyd caught his guards napping. He kicked out a window of the railroad car and leaped to the embankment below.

He was then employed by William 'The Killer' Miller in a string of bank robberies in Michigan. Fleeing the law, they arrived in Kansas City, where Miller and Nelson killed two men. Once again on the run, they robbed several banks in Kentucky.

Figuring to hide out for a while, they were stopped by police outside of Bowling Green, Ohio. Floyd killed one of the officers, and one of them killed Miller. Pretty Boy Floyd went into hiding, until Prohibition agents closed in on him. On 21 July 1931, Floyd shot his way out of a federal trap, killing Prohibition Agent Curtis Burks.

Then came an incident that truly spelled the end for 'Pretty Boy' Floyd. There is a lot of debate over Floyd's involvement, even to this day. The known facts are as follows.

Convicted bank robber Frank 'Jelly' Nash was in federal captivity. The train bearing Nash and his state and federal guards was to arrive at Union Station in Kansas City, Kansas on 17 June 1933. Nash was then to be speedily transferred to an automobile for the last leg of his journey to Leavenworth Federal Penitentiary.

As Frank Nash and his captors left the train and entered Union Station parking lot, three gunmen sprang from cover, spraying the entourage with a hail of bullets from their Thompson submachine guns. As the killers fled the scene, three policemen, a federal agent and Frank 'Jelly' Nash lay dead on the pavement.

The incident became known as the 'Kansas City Massacre.' It was the last straw in a mounting pile of criminal offenses that were, finally, to result in the FBI's licensing by the federal government to declare all-out war on interstate criminals.

Floyd was positively identified as the so-called 'brains' of the Chicago Massacre, and came to bear, like John Dillinger, the crushing weight of being 'Public Enemy Number One,' with the sure knowledge that meant his swift demise. Floyd went so far as to write to the Kansas City police, protesting his innocence. It was to no avail.

Also alleged to have taken part in the killing were gunsels Vern Miller and Adam Richetti. Motivation for the killings was never solidly established—theories posited that either it was a very badly bungled attempt to rescue Nash, or it was an execution because Nash knew too much about someone who didn't want to be investigated at any point in time.

The fact that Miller was found a month later, having been killed by torture, would seem to point to the methods of big gangs like the Capone mob, and might tilt the evidence toward the latter supposition. Richetti, who never disclosed the 'secret,' was apprehended after a shootout with police, was tried and was executed for the murders.

On 22 October 1934, FBI agents cornered Floyd at a farm in Ohio. Far from his birthplace in Oklahoma, Pretty Boy Floyd, trying to escape across a field, was cut down by lawmen's bullets. Special Agent Melvin Purvis, who had also ended John Dillinger's career, was the agent in charge of the trap.

Purvis bent over Floyd and asked him if he had really been involved in the Kansas City Massacre. Floyd said 'I didn't do it.' He died shortly thereafter.

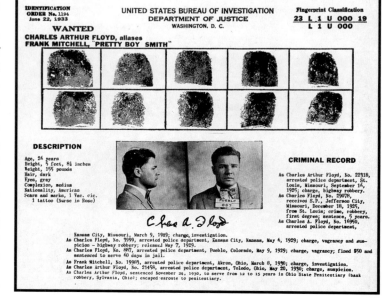

Baby Face Nelson

Here was a 'no frills' psychopath. Ostensibly, Baby Face Nelson gained his name in part because of his boyish looks. Born Lester Gillis, it is assumed that the 'Nelson' part was added to give a gangsterish cant to the rather humorous 'Baby Face' appellation.

Crude as it all seems, this was generally the way that these men—even the cleverest of them—thought. Not that his name didn't impart a certain ironic quality to him—it could, in fact, conceivably baffle those who were not yet familiar with his pathetically twisted mind.

He was born Lester M Gillis, in 1908. His boyhood spent in the streets of Chicago, he soon developed into a singularly aggressive thug. Short for his age, he seemed bent on making up for his height by being more vicious than anyone else.

In the 1920s, he found employment as an 'enforcer' in Al Capone's protection racket, but proved to be too eager to kill people. Capone, and soon, every gangster in Chicago, shunned Nelson as even more than *they* could stomach. He went out on his own, then.

Nelson was arrested for the robbery of a jewelry store in 1931, and was sent to Joliet State Prison. In less than a year, he escaped, to perpetrate a series of bank robberies in Iowa, Nebraska and Wisconsin. His cohorts in these crimes were John Chase, Eddie Green and Thomas Carroll.

He eluded the police, and joined John Dillinger when the latter escaped from Crown Point Jail. Nelson made even Dillinger nervous, but was useful, in gangland parlance, as he was an eager bank robber. On one occasion, he and Dillinger were riding in a stolen car, in March, 1934. They had an accident with another car driven by innocent bystander Theodore Kidder. When Kidder approached them to protest, Nelson shot him dead.

Then came the shootout at Little Bohemia Lodge, which is discussed more fully in the John Dillinger segment of this book. Even after the other gang members escaped, Nelson stayed behind to shoot at the federal agents. He was, in truth, stupid, escaping to another resort in the vicinity. When agents, acting on a tip, caught up with him there, Nelson stole a car and, shooting furiously as he drove away, killed Special Agent W Carter Baum.

Nelson fled to California, and doubled back to Chicago, to pick up a girl he had married in his travels, and to make contact with fellow thug John Chase. The rest of the Dillinger gang either dispersed or killed, Nelson was now Public Enemy Number One. He, his wife and Chase lay low until 27 November 1934, when FBI agents Sam Cowley and Herman Hollis found them driving on a country road near Fox River Grove, Illinois.

A running gun battle ensued, and Nelson suddenly pulled over. His wife ran into a field while he and Chase prepared for a shootout. The agents and the thugs shot at each other from cover for several minutes, and then Nelson stood up and ran at the agents, firing machine gun and maniacally yelling 'Come and get it.'

Cowley and Hollis continued shooting and wounded Nelson numerous times, but he kept coming. Both Cowley and Hollis were killed. Nelson, his body riddled with bullet wounds, stole the agents' car with the help of Chase and his wife. His escape was destined to be short lived. The next morning, police found Baby Face Nelson, the notorious gunman who was Public Enemy Number One, dead and abandoned in a ditch, some 20 miles from the scene of his suicidal gun battle with the law.

Wanted posters for 'Pretty Boy' Floyd (*at far left*) and 'Baby Face Nelson' (*below*). *Below left:* A closeup: Nelson had been, variously, with Dillinger *and* Capone, and had made even those notorious sociopaths uneasy.

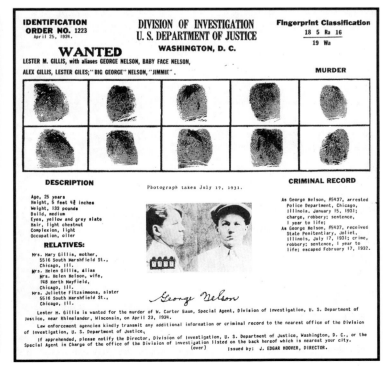

IDENTIFICATION ORDER NO. 1223
April 25, 1934.

DIVISION OF INVESTIGATION
U. S. DEPARTMENT OF JUSTICE
WASHINGTON, D. C.

Fingerprint Classification
18 5 Ra 16
19 Wa

WANTED

LESTER M. GILLIS, with aliases GEORGE NELSON, BABY FACE NELSON, ALEX GILLIS, LESTER GILES;" BIG GEORGE" NELSON, "JIMMIE".

MURDER

DESCRIPTION

Photograph taken July 17, 1931.

CRIMINAL RECORD

Age, 25 years
Height, 5 feet 4¾ inches
Weight, 133 pounds
Build, medium
Eyes, yellow and grey slate
Hair, light chestnut
Complexion, light
Occupation, oiler

RELATIVES:

Mrs. Mary Gillis, mother, 5516 South Marshfield St., Chicago, Ill.
Mrs. Helen Gillis, alias Mrs. Helen Nelson, wife, 148 North Mayfield, Chicago, Ill.
Mrs. Juliette Fitzsimmons, sister 5516 South Marshfield St., Chicago, Ill.

As George Nelson, #5437, arrested Police Department, Chicago, Illinois, January 15, 1931; charge, robbery; sentence, 1 year to life;
As George Nelson, #5437, received State Penitentiary, Joliet, Illinois, July 17, 1931; crime, robbery; sentence, 1 year to life; escaped February 17, 1932.

George Nelson

Lester M. Gillis is wanted for the murder of W. Carter Baum, Special Agent, Division of Investigation, U. S. Department of Justice, near Rhinelander, Wisconsin, on April 23, 1934.

Law enforcement agencies kindly transmit any additional information or criminal record to the nearest office of the Division of Investigation, U. S. Department of Justice.

If apprehended, please notify the Director, Division of Investigation, U. S. Department of Justice, Washington, D. C., or the Special Agent in Charge of the office of the Division of Investigation listed on the back hereof which is nearest your city.
(over)   Issued by: J. EDGAR HOOVER, DIRECTOR.

Ma Barker and Her Boys

'**M**a' Barker was borne Arizona Clark Barker in the Ozarks, and despite her dowdy appearance, managed the criminal activities of her four sons Arthur (also known as 'Doc'), Fred, Herman and Lloyd and another young man named Alvin Karpis. Though she has become well known since, she was actually hidden behind the activities of her proteges until her own violent death, when the true story of this outlaw mother came to light. In a criminal career that continued throughout the 1920s and early 1930s, the Barker-Karpis Gang terrorized the Midwest and the Plains States. Petty crime, bank robberies, murder and—eventually—kidnapping were their forte.

They were absolutely ruthless, and exhibited the peculiar inconsistencies of the criminally insane. For instance, while Ma and her boys had no compunction about killing anyone who got in their way—and even those who didn't—the boys exhibited a classic filial attachment to their mother, and she was a bit too much of a mother to them—excepting, of course, that the normal parental role in this case was subverted to the inculcation and encouragement of a recidivous criminality in the unfortunate sons, and their 'adopted' sibling, Karpis.

Ma Barker had always protected her sons. Whenever they had a youthful scrape with the law, she appeared at the police station, berating any officers who would treat her boys as if they had done something wrong. Under such 'careful nurturing,' they grew bold in doing whatever came into their heads.

They often committed crimes separately, and alternated between apparently capricious killings and planned robberies, during which they also committed a number of murders. 'Doc' killed a night watchman while trying to steal a drug shipment in 1918. Not being very bright, he was apprehended swiftly,

and was sentenced to 13 years in prison.

Lloyd robbed a post office in 1922, and, no brighter than Doc, was caught immediately and spent 25 years behind bars. Fred robbed a bank in 1926 and, no more elusive than his brothers, spent the next five years in prison. Herman Barker was apprehended for a bank robbery in 1927, immediately escaped custody and was trapped by police a short while later. Realizing that he was prison bound, Herman evidenced the true Barker mentality when he shot himself in the head.

Like Bonnie and Clyde, Dillinger and other notorious gangsters of the era, the Barkers were the subject of many a newspaper paean to 'freedom,' but the outlaws' actions really showed that they would readily subjugate others to their whims, even to the point of death, and that they themselves were so completely the prisoners of their own delusions that, rather than simply live a reasonable life, they would go to no end of trial and travail, and death and destruction, in order to satisfy their selfish and aimless urges.

When Fred Barker got out of prison in 1931, he brought with him Alvin 'Creepy' Karpis, a bank robber and gunsel that Ma Barker took a 'motherly' liking to immediately. Fred and Alvin killed a sheriff in Missouri almost immediately upon their release, and then slew the police chief of Pocahontas, Arkansas in November of that same year.

Doc Barker was also released in 1931, and he, Fred and Alvin really began to darken the Midwestern horizon when they killed two policemen and a passerby during a bank robbery in Minneapolis in December of 1932. Their robberies were many, and they murdered another policeman during a payroll stickup in 1933.

Fred and Doc killed another policeman shortly thereafter, while robbing a Federal Reserve Bank mail truck, and added personal motivation to their impetus to kill when they decided to 'get rid of' Ma's boyfriend. They simply didn't like him,

so they killed him, and of course, Ma couldn't refuse her boys.

Then, Fred and Doc decided to have their facial features and fingerprints surgically altered. The psychotic duo hired an unfortunate hack, who botched the job and paid with his life.

As seems to be inevitable with gangs, they reached a point of 'critical mass,' in which years of being on the run resulted in a desire to even more outrageously flout the law by pulling a number of big jobs, and then, as they would hope, holing up until the 'heat' died down.

They had begun to become nationally notorious when they robbed a bank in Concordia, Kansas in July of 1932. The robbery netted them $240,000, a pretty hefty sum for a daylight robbery. In June of 1933, they became kidnappers. The 'Lindbergh Law' had recently been enacted, making kidnapping a federal offense. The gang abducted brewer William A Hamm, Junior, in June of 1933, and in January of 1934, they abducted banker Edward G Bremer. The ransoms collected for these two kidnappings in the St Paul, Minnesota, area totalled $300,000.

The Barker Gang depended on a well-developed network of fellow criminals to help them hide the victims until the ransoms were paid. Within months after the second kidnapping, the FBI had apprehended and built solid conviction cases on, or killed in gun battles, dozens of suspects and their accomplices in several states.

Doc Barker had left a fingerprint at the scene of Bremer's kidnapping, and suddenly, the Barker Gang found itself in the sights of the FBI. Doc was traced to Chicago, where Special Agent Melvin Purvis, that fearsome eliminator of outlaws, apprehended him without a shot. Doc was eventually sent to Alcatraz, where he rubbed shoulders with Al Capone (and fellow gangmember Alvin Karpis), and was killed during an escape attempt in 1939.

The FBI found a map of Florida in Doc's apartment, and with it, they traced Ma Barker and son Fred to Oklawaha, Florida. Early in the morning of 16 January 1935, agents surrounded a two-story frame house on the outskirts of Oklawaha.

Upon ordering the Barkers to surrender, the FBI men received machine gun fire from a second-story window. There ensued a furious hour-long gun battle that left both Ma and Freddy Barker dead. They were both armed with submachine guns, and the story of Ma Barker made sensational headlines. Even bigger headlines were made, however, by the increasing efficiency of the FBI, and boys across the land started playing 'cops and robbers' games in which they all wanted to play the role of the heroic, FBI 'G Men.'

Alvin Karpis was captured in May, 1936. Sentenced to a life term, he was remanded to Alcatraz, joining Doc Barker in that legendary place of confinement. Karpis became very close to Al Capone, and learned to play the guitar passably well—as he admitted, on the eve of his release from jail, 33 years later.

Below opposite: **Ma and Fred Barker.** *Below:* **Alvin Karpis' capture in May 1936.** *At bottom left:* **Karpis.** *At bottom:* **Adam Richetti—associate of the Barkers, and of Pretty Boy Floyd.**

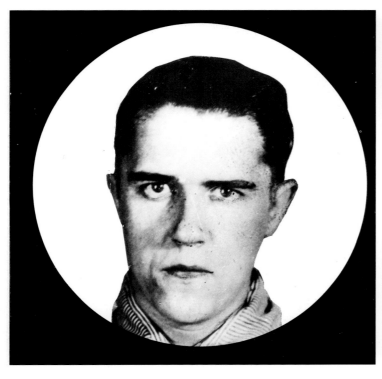

Machine Gun Kelly

George 'Machine Gun' Kelly's notorious nature was invented for him by his wife Kathryn, who sought to impress their gangster friends by inflating George's reputation. Actually, Kelly had operated for years without the 'Machine Gun' appellation, engaged in petty bootlegging and minor robberies.

Kathryn bought him a Thompson submachine gun, and mousy George obediently practiced with it until he could knock a row of walnuts off a wall at 10 feet. Kathryn, having supplied him with the prop for the persona she was inventing for him, also felt that George should step into the 'big time,' and talked him into perpetrating a kidnapping.

The kidnapping of the Lindbergh baby, and its tragic outcome, had just resulted in the passage of the Lindbergh Law, making kidnapping a federal offense with heavy penalties. The Kellys and several accomplices kidnapped wealthy Charles Urschel in the summer of 1933.

The ransome paid and the kidnappers flown, Urschel was able to help the FBI solve the case by remembering the exact times of day that airliners had flown over the cabin in which he'd been held for ransom.

Within a month, the ransome was recovered and several accomplices were rounded up. The Kellys were at large, and a sensation-seeking press had declared weak-kneed George 'Machine Gun' Kelly the most dangerous criminal alive.

He had, in fact served two prison terms for bootlegging and vagrancy. When the FBI caught up to George and Kathryn in Memphis, Tennessee, on 26 September 1933, 'Machine Gun' Kelly started using his brain and gave up.

Two versions of his arrest exist. One has it that, when an

FBI agent thrust a shotgun barrel into his midrift on a sunny street, George said, 'I've been waiting for you.' The other version is a little more dramatic: in this, the Kellys' hideout was surrounded by the FBI. When the agents 'went in after' them, George threw up his hands and said: 'Don't shoot, G Men! Don't shoot!' ('G Men' for 'government men.')

George 'Machine Gun' Kelly, and his wife and partner in crime Kathryn Kelly, received life sentences after their trial in Oklahoma City. George Kelly served time in Alcatraz, and died in Leavenworth in 1954.

Below: George 'Machine Gun' Kelly. *Below right:* Wanted poster.
Above right: George and Kathryn Kelly on trial in October 1933.
Opposite: Clyde Barrow, partner-in-crime of Bonnie Parker.

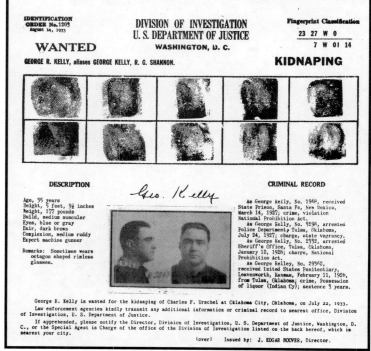

IDENTIFICATION ORDER No.1205
August 14, 1933

DIVISION OF INVESTIGATION
U. S. DEPARTMENT OF JUSTICE
WASHINGTON, D. C.

Fingerprint Classification
23 27 W 0
7 W 01 14

WANTED

GEORGE R. KELLY, aliases GEORGE KELLY, R. G. SHANNON.

KIDNAPING

DESCRIPTION

Age, 35 years
Height, 5 feet, 9½ inches
Weight, 177 pounds
Build, medium muscular
Eyes, blue or gray
Hair, dark brown
Complexion, medium ruddy
Expert machine gunner

Remarks: Sometimes wears octagon shaped rimless glasses.

CRIMINAL RECORD

As George Kelly, No. 1968, received State Prison, Santa Fe, New Mexico, March 14, 1927; crime, violation National Prohibition Act.
As George Kelly, No. 5298, arrested Police Department, Tulsa, Oklahoma, July 24, 1927; charge, state vagrancy.
As George Kelly, No. 2932, arrested Sheriff's Office, Tulsa, Oklahoma, January 12, 1928; charge, National Prohibition Act.
As George Kelley, No. 29962, received United States Penitentiary, Leavenworth, Kansas, February 11, 1928, from Tulsa, Oklahoma; crime, Possession of liquor (Indian Cy); sentence 3 years.

George R. Kelly is wanted for the kidnaping of Charles F. Urschel at Oklahoma City, Oklahoma, on July 22, 1933.
Law enforcement agencies kindly transmit any additional information or criminal record to nearest office, Division of Investigations, U. S. Department of Justice.
If apprehended, please notify the Director, Division of Investigation, U. S. Department of Justice, Washington, D. C., or the Special Agent in Charge of the office of the Division of Investigation listed on the back hereof, which is nearest your city.

(over)   Issued by: J. EDGAR HOOVER, Director.

Bonnie and Clyde

Bonnie Parker and Clyde Barrow were the most notorious gangster 'couple' in the annals of crime. Clyde Barrow began his criminal career, oddly enough, with keeping a rental car past its 'due back' date. He was forgiven the offense on the basis of his youth and his somewhat absent-minded sensitivity. Unfortunately, this was beginning of a downward spiral into full criminality, as he began to seek sustenance through outlaw means that he could not, or would not obtain for himself.

He was a sensitive, but warped individual, whose primary weakness was a monumental self-centeredness that dictated a life of crime as opposed to honest work—which he felt was 'beneath' him. Clyde and his brother Buck engaged in a number of safe cracking jobs in the late 1920s, most of which were perpetrated in the vicinity of Denton, Texas, just south of 'the Panhandle.'

Detained by the police on several occasions, Clyde, Buck and two accomplices continued in their inexpert ways. On more than one occasion, they simply had to leave the booty behind, lacking the expertise to open strong box or safe that contained it.

Finally, in October of 1929, the gang robbed a garage, literally stealing the safe *in toto*, in the hopes that they could crack it open at their hiding place. The stolen car recklessly driven by Clyde crashed into a curb and the robbers were apprehended by pistol-wielding police. Clyde Barrow had fled the scene on foot, only to be apprehended later on

warrants pending in the towns of Sherman and Waco. Clyde served two years in prison on these charges.

He had, however, just met the woman who was to be partner in crime. Both of them were already married, and undivorced, but estranged from their spouses. Bonnie Parker, like Clyde Barrow, had been the focus of her family's attention. Pampered and exhibitionistic, she nevertheless attempted to persuade Clyde to 'go straight,' writing him letters while he was in prison that underscored the error of his ways.

Clyde's unbending pride won her over, however, and swept along on a stream of passion, she was his ready accomplice when Clyde got out of jail. Her terrible temper seemed ready made for a gun moll, and even though terrified of firearms while a child, she readily assumed the role of a gun-toting—and gun-using—female thug.

Clyde got out of prison on 2 February 1932. His revulsion to manual labor was such that he had a fellow convict chop two of his toes off so that he would be unable to work in the prison 'yard.' Thus, he returned home a cripple. By this time fancying himself a gangster, he took up the life of the outlaw. After a brief and unsuccessful attempt to hold down a job, he involved Bonnie in their first crime as a couple.

On 20 March 1932, they engineered a robbery in the vicinity of Kaufman, Texas, and were caught in the act. Fleeing the scene in a stolen car, they soon had to flee on foot when the car became entrapped in a bog.

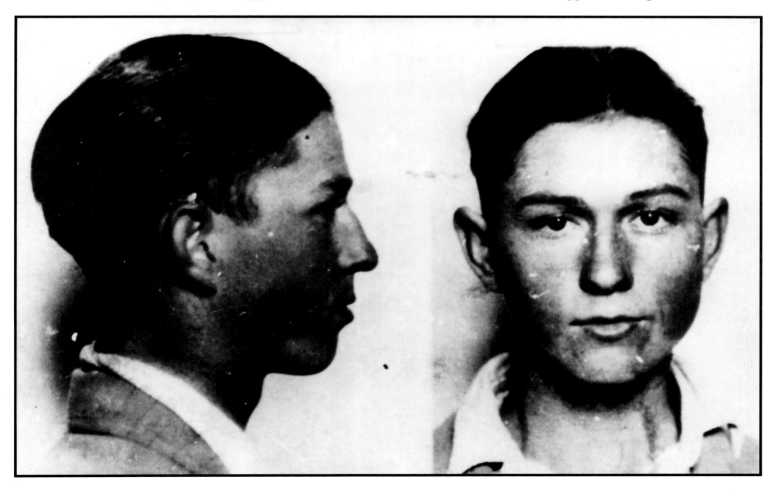

It was rumored that Bonnie was captured and spent a month in jail, while Clyde and an accomplice continued the crime spree. At any rate, the notoriety of Clyde Barrow and his petite blonde (though Bonnie often dyed her hair) partner soon began to blacken newspaper headlines.

Clyde was involved in his first murder 27 April 1932. The victims were the parents of one of Clyde's childhood friends, and they died when Clyde and his accomplices tried to rob the couple's music store. This was to be the beginning of a long string of murders for Clyde — so much so that, when Bonnie's mother insisted that he had not been involved in the music store murder, against all evidence that he was, she said '…since he later killed so many men, and admitted the killings to us, I believe he told the truth about the…affair.'

Bonnie and Clyde terrorized the Southwest thereafter, pulling robberies with one or two accomplices, and every so often kidnapping a police officers, sometimes as a hostage, and sometimes 'just for the heck of it,' almost always turning their victim loose far from where they picked him up.

One evening in the fall of the same year that the music store murders had occurred, Clyde and three of his 'boys,' including number one accomplice Raymond Hamilton, stopped by a barn dance. They'd been drinking quite a bit and a debate broke out as to whether they, wanted men all of them, should go to a public function like a barn dance.

A county sheriff and his deputy approached them to see what the argument was about. Barrow and his gang panicked and killed the officers with a hail of lead. It was typical of the almost inadvertent way in which the Barrow gang

Bonnie and Clyde 'press releases.' *Below, left to right:* **Clyde; Bonnie; Bonnie and Clyde posing; Faye Dunaway and Warren Beatty as Bonnie and Clyde in the 1967 movie, *Bonnie and Clyde*.**

committed its many murders; in the heat of the moment, human life lost all its value for them, so caught up were they in their own objectives, no matter how petty.

'Bonnie and Clyde' had by now really caught on with the popular press, and news of Clyde Barrow and Bonnie Parker included quite a few exploits that were not really theirs. A sort of 'Robin Hood' fever of positive sentiment for the pair and their gang had developed among the populace — even in the face of the fact that increasing numbers of innocent citizens were being killed in robberies (and 'accidents' such as the barn dance fiasco) by these lunatics.

Adding to this dramatization of their exploits were the notes and comic photographs of themselves that Bonnie and Clyde supplied to newspapers and police correspondents throughout the South and Southwest: it all amounted to a self-glorifying publicity campaign that actually gained the Barrow Gang an untold number of accomplices, in terms of people who would not tell police when they'd sighted Bonnie and Clyde, and also in terms of people who would hide them in their houses for a few days.

Traps were set, ambushes laid and all points bulletins sent out over the wires in order to snare the Barrow Gang, but Clyde's peculiar sixth sense seemed to warn him whenever the trap was about to close, and he and his gang invariably effected a disappearance from the vicinity, sometimes, as we have already said, kidnapping an officer of the law for 'insurance,' only to set him free hundreds of miles from his place of origin.

Raymond Hamilton had another yen to dance one night in Michigan, and, waxing talkative with his partner, soon found himself in jail facing extradition to Texas, where he was given a 263-year prison sentence for his exploits.

At this time, WD Jones, a thrill-seeking 16-year-old, joined

the Barrow Gang, against Clyde's wishes. Immediately the boy killed a man while stealing his car, and was to establish a career of murders and maimings quite in keeping with the Barrow Gang's *modus operandi*.

Shortly, Clyde's brother Buck was released from prison, and though he promised to go straight—and his wife Blanche implored him to do so—he insisted on visiting Clyde. While there, Clyde, WD and Bonnie became embroiled in a gun battle with police, and Buck and Blanche—*ipso facto*—were named as accomplices. In their escape from the battle, they left two dead policemen behind them.

Buck, though he'd only wanted to visit his brother, had been dragged down by Clyde's madness, and, by sheer association with the most desperate criminal of his day, was also a candidate for the electric chair.

It might be assumed that there was an objective in all of this—even the craziest thugs always seemed to have profit in some way, shape or form in mind, as an adjunct to their actions. For Clyde Barrow, though, it was a romantic venture. He was willing to sacrifice others on the altar of his own vision of spending his life in flight, as a fugitive—much like the adolescent Arthur Rimbaud's warped ideal of the artist as burnt-out case, perhaps 30 years before.

The truth was that a really 'big' heist for the early Barrow gang might have amounted to $100. In the drama of the chase, the gang was apt to change its appearance, dyeing their hair, changing clothes, and so on.

Clyde drove like a maniac, always and ever—and it was a fact that got the gang into more than one kind of difficulty. One of the more serious incidents involved a washed-out bridge that Clyde saw too late, and an accident ensued in which Bonnie was very badly burned. This resulted in a period of quiescence for Bonnie and Clyde, as they hid out at

a tourist camp near Fort Smith, Arkansas. Clyde stayed by Bonnie's side, and even hired a nurse to tend her.

During this time, Buck and WD raised the gang's spending money by pulling bank robberies in the vicinity. The inevitable happened, and the two robbers became involved in a gun battle with police, following a traffic accident en route to a heist. On 26 June 1933, they headed for a tourist camp at Great Bend, Kansas, in order to leave the now-charged atmosphere of their Arkansas hideout.

In mid-July, Bonnie was able to travel, and this vicinity now also 'hot' because of still more robberies that WD and Buck had pulled, the gang drove en masse to Fort Dodge, Iowa and robbed three filling stations. They then drove to Platte City, Missouri, and rented two tourist cabins with a garage between them. The neighbors were suspicious, and, before long, the Platte City police had called in reinforcements to help them 'take' the Barrow Gang.

Blocking the garage with an armored car, a veritable army of policemen surprised the sleeping gang. Clyde poured machine gun fire into the armored car, wounding and officer inside it, and forcing the police to move it for the safety of the men inside. Throwing open the garage doors, the Barrow gang escaped in a hail of bullets, with Buck being badly wounded and Blanche getting splinters in her eyes from the car windows, which were exploding from the force of flying lead. Once again, Clyde's eccentric, high speed driving managed to lose the pursuing posse.

A day and a half later, they pulled into a field near Dexter, Iowa, to make plans for the future. With a Buck dying, Bonnie still suffering from her burns and Blanche blinded by the glass splinters in her eyes, the situation was grim. They'd left bloody bandages all along the way, at regular intervals, wherever they'd stopped for a breather; further, Clyde and

WD went into Dexter to pick up food, and while there, WD stole a second car for them, to make travelling with the invalids easier.

Clyde made up his mind to drive Buck back to Texas, as he was not long for this world, and they knew that his mother would want to see him before he died.

It was night, and they'd decided to head back home with Buck, when a large posse burst out of the brush upon them. There followed a wild melee of shooting, in which Clyde was wounded while trying to drive the getaway car, and ran it onto a stump.

Their second car was destroyed by gunfire, so they had to flee on foot, WD and Bonnie hiding in the thickets and Clyde in search of a car to steal.

Buck, too hurt to make it on foot, insisted on being left behind, and loyal Blanche stayed with him. He'd been shot many, many times by now, yet lived in custody for six more days. Blanche was also, of course, now 'one of the Barrow Gang,' and she received a prison term. Their capture, however, served to aid the others' escape.

Clyde had found a car on the other side of a nearby bridge, but the posse was waiting for him, and had wrecked it to block his escape that way. Somehow, he made it to Bonnie and WD—both bleeding and wounded in the thickets.

With the posse on the high ground, they had to ford a river. The posse saw them when they were halfway across, and Bonnie was wounded again in the ensuing fusillade.

On the other side, with the river between them and the posse, they stole a car from a family of farmers, and WD drove them as far as Polk City, Iowa, where they stole a faster car. With only a damaged and useless pistol and no medical supplies, the desperadoes headed for Denver, but upon reading a newspaper account that claimed they were already in Denver, they turned around and headed in the opposite direction. They hid out in wooded ravines and side roads for the next few weeks, until their wounds began to heal. As soon as Clyde could drive again, WD left them, and Bonnie and Clyde, sensing that the end was near, headed for Texas, desiring to be close to home when the end came.

Afraid of being trapped by police while staying inside a house, they lived entirely in the car. Bonnie could hardly walk, still suffering from her burns. They visited their folks on 7 September 1933, and were completely caught up with 'being on the run.' They hadn't been inside a house for months. They stayed on, visiting their folks often, through November.

During an arranged meeting in a backwoods lane, the police once again descended on Bonnie and Clyde. Waiting for them in a separate car, their two mothers witnessed their outlaw children trading shots with the police while speeding away amid the ricocheting bullets.

Both Bonnie and Clyde were wounded in the knees by the same bullet. Amazingly, neither even knew of their new wounds until Clyde fell while trying to open a gate.

They stole another car as the tires on their present car were flattened by bullet damage. Four hundred miles later, they stole a third car. Bleeding heavily by that time, they headed for Oklahoma, where they received medical attention and stole yet a fourth car. Clyde determined to take revenge on Sheriff Smoot Schmid, who had laid the trap for them. Clyde's motivation was that he and Bonnie's mothers could have been killed in the gunfire, and 'Schmid should have thought of that.'

Amazingly, the man that police throughout the Southwest were hunting stalked the Sheriff's house for nights on end, and stalked the Dallas County Jail, hoping to get a crack at Schmid. Bonnie's mother talked him out of his vendetta, eventually. By now, WD Smith was behind bars, and was busily dictating his memoirs as a former member of the Barrow Gang.

They stayed in and around Dallas until mid-December, 1933. Clyde had by now adopted a disguise for going into town: he wore a woman's wig and makeup, so that he and Bonnie—by now probably the most publicized faces in the Southwest—appeared to be just 'two girls out for an afternoon.'

In truth, they could not rest or stop anywhere for long. The police and citizenry hunted and feared them as they had no other criminals in recent memory. They continued their ways, holding up five-and-dime stores, salesmen, money collectors, gas stations and on one occasion, a refinery. By now, Bonnie was suffering from arthritis, brought on by their injuries and exposed way of living.

On 16 January 1934, Clyde broke Raymond Hamilton out of Eastham Prison Farm, and along with Hamilton came five other escapees. James Mullens, a friend of Hamilton's, had promised to contact Clyde with the plans for the breakout if Hamilton would pay him $1000.

After his escape, Hamilton therefore had a thousand-dollar debt to pay. One of Raymond's fellow escapees, Henry Methvyn, joined the gang, and he, Clyde and Raymond robbed a bank at Lancaster, Texas, for $2400, giving the men $800 apiece. Raymond wanted more money than that, so embarked on a number of robberies independently.

Clyde didn't trust Raymond's girlfriend, Alice, and seeing Raymond's ambition, grew to distrust him also. Soon, Raymond had paid Mullens off, and Bonnie, Clyde, Raymond, Alice and Henry headed north to escape the increasing police pressure in Texas. They settled for awhile in Indiana, where the friction between the Barrow Gang and Raymond and Alice grew to the breaking point, and in fact, the partnership ended acrimoniously.

Bonnie, Clyde and Henry headed back to Texas. Near Easter time, the three were taking their leisure near a road in the vicinity of Grapevine, Texas, when they were approached by police officers. Clyde had intended to kidnap the policemen, but Henry, being an escaped convict, panicked and mowed them down with machine gun fire.

They fled to Oklahoma, where, less than a week later, they killed Constable Cal Campbell at Commerce, and kidnapped that municipality's police chief, Percy Boyd. They let the chief go with the admonition to tell the world that Bonnie Parker was *not* in the habit of smoking cigars.

Bonnie and Clyde were not long for this world. They planned to set up housekeeping in Louisiana on property owned by Henry Methvyn's father, but on 23 May 1934, as Bonnie and Clyde were returning from a jaunt to a nearby town, they came upon Henry's father, who was ostensibly fixing a flat tire for his truck, parked beside the road.

Clyde parked parallel to the truck to see if he could help, and shortly, another truck came over the crest of a hill, blowing its horn for Clyde to move his car out of the way. Clyde pulled in front of the Methvyn truck, and started to back up.

At that moment, a small army of police officers, led by the colorful ex-Texas Ranger Frank Hamer, opened fire with machine guns from their camouflaged positions in the ditch beside the road. This time, the Barrow luck did not hold.

Without returning a single shot, Bonnie and Clyde died that May morning, riddled with bullets in a stolen car, never again to rob a gas station or a bank, and never again to be fugitives from the law.

Below opposite: A wanted poster. Courtesy of Texas Ranger buff Bob Hendley *(below, clockwise from left):* Ambush leaders Frank Hamer (black hat), Sheriff Henderson Jordan and Bob Alcorn; Bonnie and Clyde's arsenal; and 'the end,' 23 May 1934.

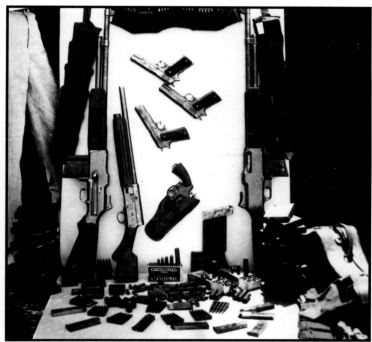

INDEX

Accardo, Antonino 'Joe Batters' 24
Adonis, Joe 56, 58, 60, 62, 64–65, 68, 71, 75
Adonis Social Club 25
Ahern, Michael 24, 48, 50
Aiello, Andrew 31
Aiello, Dominick 31
Aiello, Joseph 31–33, 35–36, 68
Aiello, Tony 31
Alcatraz Island Federal Prison 50, 51, 52, 53, 87
Alcorn, Bob 93
Alliance Distributors 74
Alo, Jimmy 'Blue Eyes' 67
Alogno, Lorenzo 32
Alterie, Louie 16, 21
Amatuna, Samuzzo 'Samoots' 16, 24
Anastasia, Albert 58, 68, 73, 75–76, 77
Annenberg, Moses 66–67
Anselmi, Albert 16, 21, 24–26, 28–29, 31, 37–38
Anton, Theodore 'The Greek' 29–30
Atlanta Federal Penitentiary 50
Atlantian, The 53
Atlantic City, New Jersey 38, 66
Attlomionte, Diego 32

Bailey, Attorney General Carl E 75
Baldelli, Ecola 'The Eagle' 24–25
Balitzer, Mildred 77
Balitzer, Peter 'Harris' 76–77
'Bananas, Joe' 67–68
Barbizon Plaza Hotel 67, 77
Barker, Arizona Clark see Barker, Ma
Barker, Arthur 'Doc' 86–87
Barker, Fred 86–87, 86
Barker, Herman 86
Barker-Karpis Gang 80, 86–87
Barker, Lloyd 86
Barker, Ma 38, 86–87, 87
Barko, Louis 28
Barrow, Blanche 91–92
Barrow, Buck 89, 91–92
Barrow, Clyde 4, 88–93, 89–93
Barrow Gang 80, 86, 88–93
Bascone, Vito 25
Basile, Frank 40, 44
Batista, Fulgencio 74
Battery Park, Manhattan 67
Baum, Special Agent W Carter 85
Beattie, Warren 91
Belcastro, James 'Bomber' 22
Bell, Jean 78
Bendix, Joe 77
Berkman, Meyer 74, 76
Berman, Otto 'Abbadabba' 72–73
Bertche, Barney 31
Betillo, 'Little Davie' 74–77
Better Government Association of Chicago and Cook County 26
Big Bill, The 29
'Big Fellow' see Capone, Alphonse
Biltmore Hotel, Los Angeles 32
Biltmore Hotel, Manhattan 60
Biograph Theater 83, 83
Birger, Charlie 29–31
Birger Gang 29
Bitz, Bitzi 65

Black Hand 9–10
'Black Sox' scandal 58–59, 59
Blackstone Hotel 70
Blaudins, Giovanni 32
Bloom, Samuel 65
Board of Trade Building 26–27
Boccia, Ferdinand 'The Shadow' 74
'Bootlegger's conference' 66
Bonanno, Joseph see 'Bananas, Joe'
Bonnie and Clyde see Parker, Bonnie and Barrow, Clyde; also see Barrow Gang
Bonnie and Clyde (motion picture) 91
'Boss of Bosses' 60, 68, 70
Boston Tea Party 50
Boyd, Police Chief Percy 93
Breitel, Investigator Charles 74
Bremer, Edward G 87
Bromfman, Sam 62
Brown, Florence 'Cokey Flo' 77
Brothers, Leo Vincent 44
Brooklyn, New York 6, 58, 76
Brooklyn Truant School 54
Brooks, Joey 43
Bronx, The 68–69, 72, 76
Brown, Al see Alphonse Capone
Buchalter, Louis see Lepke, Charlie
Bucher, George 'Sport' 18
'Bug and Meyer Gang' 58
Burke, Fred 37–38
Burks, Prohibition Agent Curtis 84
Burnham, Illinois 12
'Buy-Money Bank' 56

Calabrian Carbonari 6
Camilla, Frank 14
Camorra see Neapolitan Camorra
Campagna, Louis 'Little New York' 32–33, 52
Campbell, Constable Cal 93
Capitol Wines and Spirits, Inc 74
Capone, Albert Francis 'Sonny' 9, 25
Capone, Alphonse 'Al' 7–9, 14–15, 17–25, 27–28, 30–38, 39, 40, 42–44, 46–48, 47, 50, 50, 52–53, 52, 56, 64, 67–68, 70–72, 76–77, 85, 87
Capone, Frank 19
Capone, Gabriel 6, 15
Capone Gang 22, 28–29, 40, 43–44, 48
Capone, Mae 9, 25, 52
Capone, Mafalda 38
Capone, Matt 15
Capone, Ralph 'Bottles' 15, 22, 39, 40–42, 48, 50
Capone, Teresa 6, 15
Capone soup kitchen 45
Carbonari see Calabrian Carbonari
Carlstrom, State's Attorney Oscar 26
Carroll, James see Ralph Capone
Carroll, Thomas 85
Carter, Assistant District Attorney Eunice 74
Caruso, Angie 69
Caruso, Enrico 14
'Castellamarese War' 66
Castiglia, Francesco see Costello, Frank
Celano's Restaurant 77–78
Central National Bank 81

Central Park Hotel 65
Chapman, Lyle 40
Chase, John 85
Cheech, Frankie 58, 68, 71
Chicago Candy Jobber's Union 32
Chicago Crime Commission 40
Chicago Evening American 48
Chicago Heights 15
Chicago Musical College 14
Chicago Police Department 32
'Chicago's Arch-Criminal' see Dion O'Banion
Chicago White Sox see 'Black Sox' scandal
Cicero, Illinois 14, 19, 20, 26–28, 42
Cinderella, Dominic 32
Citron, Anna see Lansky, Anna
Claridge Hotel 62
Clark, James 36
Clark, Russell 80
Clements, Hilary 29
Cleveland Boy's Town 52, 53
Cleveland Police Academy 52
Cleveland Police Department 52
Cloonan, Barney 40
'Clown', The 46
Cole, Investigator Harry 74
Coll, Vincent 'Mad Dog' 69–70, 72
Collins, Chief of Police Morgan A 19, 21
Colosimo, 'Big Jim' 9–14, 17, 19
Colosimo's Cafe 10, 14
Commerce, Oklahoma 93
Concordia, Kansas 87
Converse, Special Agent Clarence 42
Coney Island, New York 68
Congress Hotel 70
Conway, Detective Michael 24
Cook County Jail 50
Cook County Sheriff's Department 19
Coolidge, US President Calvin 33–34, 34
Corrigan, Phil 18
Costello, Frank 55–56, 56, 58, 64, 71, 74–75
Coughlin, John 'Bathhouse' 9
Coughlin, Mae see Capone, Mae
Covington, Kentucky 73
Cowan, Louis 22
Cowley, Sam 85
Crowe, Alderman Dorsey 30
Crowe, Illinois State's Attorney Robert E 26–27, 29, 33–34
Crown Point, Indiana 'escape-proof' jail 82, 85
Crutchfield, William 21
Cuba 60, 74
Cuiringione, Tommy 21
Cummings, Attorney General Homer 83
Cuneo, Secretary to the State's Attorney Lawrence 34

Daily Mirror 70
Daily News 40
Daily Racing Form 66
Dalitz, Moe 62, 71
Dallas County Jail 92
Dannenberg, WC 10
D'Andrea, Phil 22, 50, 52
Dawes, Charles G 26

De Grazio, Orchell 32
de Mora, Vincenzo see McGurn, 'Machine Gun' Jack
Democratic National Convention 71
Dempsey/Firpo heavyweight title match 60
Deneen, Senator Charles S 33–34
De Niro, Robert 46
Denton, Texas 89
Dever, Mayor William E 18–20, 29, 30
Dewey, Special Prosecutor Thomas 72, 73–78
Dexter, Iowa 91
'Diamond, Legs' see Nolan, John 73
Dillinger Gang 80–83, 85
Dillinger, John 80–86, 81–82
Doherty, Jim 20
Drucci, Vincent 'Schemer' 16, 21–22, 24, 28–29, 30
Druggan, Terry 16, 40, 52
Druggan-Lake Gang 16
Ducore's Drug Store 77
Dunaway, Faye 91
Dunbar, JV see Frank Ries

Eastern Penitentiary 38–40
Eastern Seaboard 62, 64
Eastham Prison Farm 92
Eastman, 'Monkeyface' 7
Egan, William 'Shorty' 18
Egan's Rats Gang 37
Eisen, Maxie 28
Elder, Trustee Morris
Eller, 'Boss' 34
Ellis, Oliver 42
Erickson, Frank 65, 67
Esposito, Joseph 'Diamond Joe' 34
Esposito's Bella Napoli Cafe 28

FBI 82–84, 87
FBI agents 83–85, 87–88
Federal Bureau of Investigation see FBI
Federal Reserve Bank 86
Federated Protestant Churches 10
Ferraro, Joseph 36
Ferrigno, Steve 68
Ferry, Cornelius 'Needles' 25
Fink, Albert 50
First National Bank of Chicago 81
Fischetti, Charlie 19, 22
Fitzmorris, City Controller Charles 34
Fitzpatrick, Mac 10
Five Pointers Gang 7
Flegenheimer, Arthur see Schultz, Dutch
Floyd, Charles Arthur see Floyd, 'Pretty Boy'
Floyd, 'Pretty Boy' 84, 84
Foley, Mitters 28
Forest View, Illinois 27
Fort Smith, Arkansas 91
Fotre, John 50
Four Deuces, The 12, 14–15, 19–20
Fox River Grove, Illinois 85
Frechette, Evelyn 'Billie' 83
Frederico, James 'Jimmy' 74, 77
Freeman, Mrs Clyde 28
Friel, Tom 40
Fuld, Investigator Stanley 74
Fulton Fish Market 74

Funkhauser, Police Commissioner Metellus 10, 12
Futtrell, Governor J Marion 75

'G Men' see FBI agents
Gagliano, Gaetano 'Tom' 68
Gallo, Willie 74
Gambino, Carlo 58
Gardner, Bill 40
Garment District, Manhattan 58, 64
Genna, Angelo 16, 22, 24–25
Genna, Jim 16, 21
Genna, Mike 16, 24
Genna, Pete 16
Genna, Sam 16
Genna, Tony 16, 24
Gennas, 'The Terrible' 15–16, 18, 20–21, 24, 31
Genovese, Vito 58, 60, 62, 67–68, 71, 74, 78, 79
Giancana, Sam 'Mooney' 24
Giblin, Vincent 46
Gillis, Lester see Nelson, 'Baby Face'
Giunta, John 'Hop Toad' 36–38
Goddard, Dr Herbert M 40
Goldstein, Bummy 25
Goodman, Max 55
Goodman Hat Company 55
'Gordon, Waxey' 38, 56, 59–60, 65, 73, 77
Grabiner, Joe 'Jew Kid' 10
Granady, Octavius 34
Grand Central Building, The 68
Grand Central Station, Chicago 9
Grapevine, Texas 93
Great Bend, Kansas 91
Great Depression 40, 67
Green, Eddie 85
Grimes, Investigator Charles 74
Gullet, 'Chicken Harry' 10
Gusenberg, Frank 36–37
Gusenberg, Pete 36–37
Guzik, Alma 15
Guzik, Harry 15, 22
Guzik, Jake 20, 22, 42, 48, 50, 52

Hamer, Frank 93, 93
Hamilton, John 80
Hamilton, Raymond 90, 92
Hamilton, Raymond; Alice, girlfriend of 92
Hamm, William Jr 87
Hampton Farms Penitentiary 55
Hanley, Edward 26
Harlem, New York City 56
Harms, Aaron 25
Hart, James 25
Harvard Inn 8–9
Hasmiller, Harry 18
Hastings, Mary 9
Hayes, Judge Howard 20
Hawthorne Inn 19, 38
Hawthorne Race Track 28
Hawthorne Restaurant 28
Hawthorne Smoke Shop 20, 28–30, 43, 48, 50
Healy, Detective Dan 30
Hearst newspaper chain 66–67
Heitler, Mike 'de Pike' 14, 22, 44
Helmar Social Club 72
Hendley, Bob 93
Herbert, Frank 32
Heyer, Adam 36–37

Hines, Jimmy 71
Hodgins, Special Agent William 42, 46–48
Hogan, Investigator Frank 74
Holley, Sheriff Lillian 82
Hollis, FBI Agent Herman 85
Hoover, US President Herbert 36, 66, 70
Hoover, FBI Director J Edgar 52, 73, 83
Hot Springs, Arkansas 30, 73, 74, 75
Hotel Lexington 36, 42, 46, 50
Hotel Metropole 22, 22, 30–31, 36
Hotel Sherman 30
Howard, Joe 20
Howard, Joseph 'Ragtime' 25
Hubacek, Charlie 29, 30
Humphries, Murray 'The Camel' 24
Hunt, Sam 'Golf Bag' 22, 43, 52

Indiana City State Penitentiary 80
Indianapolis, Indiana 80
International Metal Polishers Union 64
Irey, IRS Enforcement Branch Chief Elmer 40–42
Ison, 'Big Joe' 72
Italian Guardia 78
Italo-American Union 35–36, 38, 70

Jack & Charlie's 21 Club 62
Jacobs, Benny 28
Jacobs, Jesse 74
Jamerico, Numio 32
Jersey Palisades (New Jersey) 60
Joliet State Prison 26–27, 85
John Torrio Association, The 6
Johnson, Enoch 'Nucky' 62, 64–66, 73
Johnson, US Attorney George EQ 48, 50
Jones, WD 90–92
Jordan, Sheriff Henderson 93
'Jules the Commissar' 73

Kansas City, Kansas 84
'Kansas City Massacre' 84
Kansas City Police 84
Karp, Abe 74, 76
Karpis, Alvin 'Creepy' 38, 86–87, 87
Kashelleck, Jim 'Clark' 36
Kastel, 'Dandy' Phil 71, 74
Kaufman, Julius 43
Kaufman, Texas 89
Keane, Morrie 18
Kelly, George see Kelly, 'Machine Gun'
Kelly, Kathryn 88, 88
Kelly, 'Machine Gun' 88, 88
Kelly, Paul 8
Kenna, Michael 'Hinky Dink' 9, 32
Kidder, Theodore 85
King, Mike 40
'King of Beer' see Schultz, Dutch
'King of the Jersey Coast' see Johnson, Enoch
Klenha, Mayor Joseph 19–20
Knox, Colonel Frank 40
Koncil, Lefty 28–30

'Lady in Red, The Mysterious' see Sage, Anna
LaGuardia, Senator and Mayor

Fiorello 72–73
Lahart, Marty 40
Lake, Frank 16, 40
Lake County Jail 22
Lancaster, Texas 92
Landau, Abe 73
Landesman, Jeanette 37
Lansky, Anna 66–67
Lansky, Meyer 56, 56, 60, 62, 64, 66–71, 73–75
Lanza, 'Socks' 74
La Presta, Lawrence 32
Leahy, William 50
Leathers, Billie 10
Leavenworth Federal Penitentiary 40, 84, 88
Leeson, Joe 40
Lenin, Vladimir Ilich 40
Lepito, Michael see Malone, Special Agent Michael
Lepke, Charlie 58, 64, 67, 71, 76
Lercara Friddi, Sicily 54
Levee District, Chicago 10, 12
Levine, Hymie 'Loudmouth' 22
Levine, Red 68
Levy, George Morton 76–77
Liguori, Ralph 'The Pimp' 74, 76
Lima, Ohio County Jail 80
Lincoln, President Abraham 83
Lindbergh baby 88
'Lindbergh Law,' The 87–88
Lingle, Jake 43–44
'Little Bohemia' resort hotel 83, 85
Little Caesar 22–23
'Little Italy,' Chicago 18, 24, 31
Little Italy Cafe 32
Little Rock, Arkansas 75
Loesch, Chicago Crime Commission President Frank 36
Lolordo, Joseph 36–37
Lolordo, Pasquale 36
Lombardo, Tony 22, 24, 31–32, 36
Lo Mantio, Angelo 32
London Chemist Drugstore 72
Lonergan, Richard 'Peg Leg' 25
Long, Huey 'Kingfish' 71
Lord's Prayer, The 10
Lower East Side, Manhattan 8, 54–55, 62, 77
Lucania, Antonio 54–55
Lucania (Luciano) Gang 62, 64
Lucania, Rosalie 54–55
Lucania, Salvatore see Luciano, Charlie 'Lucky'
Lucchese, Tommy 'Three Finger Brown' 64, 67–69, 75
Lucia, Felice 24
Luciano, Charlie 'Lucky' 4, 9, 22, 24, 36, 38, 48, 54–62, 62, 64–78, 76, 78, 81
Luciano, Lucky see Luciano Charlie 'Lucky'
Lundin, Fred 19
'Lupo the Wolf' see Saietta, Ignazio
Lyle, Judge John H 44, 46, 48

McCook, Justice Philip J 76–77
McErlane, Frank 16, 18, 24, 43
McFall, Danny 18
McGoorty, Chicago Chief Justice John P 46
McGurn, 'Machine Gun' Jack 24, 32,

38, 52
McSwiggin, Sergeant Anthony 27–28
McSwiggin, Assistant State's Attorney William H 20, 26–27
Madden, Tax Intelligence Chief Arthur 48
Maddox, Claude 38
Madigan, Harry 27
Madison Square, Manhattan 71
Mafia see Sicilian Mafia
Makely, Charles 80
Malone, New York 73
Malone, Special Agent Michael 42
Mangano, Lawrence 22
Mangano, Philip 62
Mangano, Vincent 62
Manhattan 4, 56, 64, 71, 75–76
Manhattan Melodrama 83
Maranzano, Salvatore 48, 60, 62, 64, 66–70, 72
Marinelli, Albert 71
Marks, Willie 36
Masseria, Giuseppe 'Joe the Boss' 36, 48, 60, 62, 64, 66–70, 77
Mattingly, Lawrence P 50
May, John 36–37
Meeghan, George 18
Memphis, Tennessee 88
Merlo, Mike 21, 22
Methvyn Farm, Louisiana 93
Methvyn, Henry 92–93
Methvyn, Henry; father of 93
Miami Beach Bank 42
Michigan State Penitentiary 38
Miller, Vern 84
Miller, William 'The Killer' 84
Miranda, Mike 68
Mineo, Al 36, 68
Miro, Henry 72
Modgilewsky, Jules see 'Jules the Commissar'
Molaska Corp 74
Mondi, Jimmy 50
Moore, Dr Joseph 52
Morals Squad 10, 12
Moran Gang 30, 36–37, 64
Moran, George 'Bugs' 16, 22, 24, 28–31, 37–38, 43–44, 52
Morello, Pietro 'The Clutching Hand' 36, 68
Moresco, Joe 10
Moretti, Willie 58, 65
Morgenthau, Secretary of the Treasury Henry 73
Morici, Agostino 25
Morici, Antonio 25
Mount Olivet Cemetery 52
Mullens, James 92
Muni, Paul 23
'Murder, Incorporated' 76
Murray, Paddy 28
Mussolini, Benito 25, 64

Nash, Frank 'Jelly' 84
Nash, Thomas 40, 48
Naples, Italy 6
Napoli, Tony 46
Neapolitan Camorra 6
Nelson, 'Baby Face' 82, 85, 85
Nerone, Giuseppe 16, 24
Ness, Betty 53
Ness, Bobby 53

Ness, Federal Agent Eliot 40, *41*, 44, 46, 52–53
Newberry, Ted 36
New Brighton Dance Hall 7
New Englander Social and Dramatic Club 7
New Jersey 58–59, 64, 73–74
New Orleans, Louisiana 71, 73
Newport, Kentucky 73
New York City Police Commissioner's Office 64
New York City Police Department 71
New York Harbor *6*
'Night of the Sicilian Vespers' 70
Nitti, Frank 'The Enforcer' 22, 42
Nolan, John 'Legs Diamond' 73
Nugent, 'Crane Neck' 38
Nuovo Villa Tamaro Restaurant 68

O'Banion, Dion 15–16 *17*, 18, 20–21, 24, 28
O'Banion Gang 15, 36
O'Berta, 'Dingbat' 43
O'Brien, WW 28
O'Conner, Jerry 18
O'Conner, Chief Detective William 32
O'Donnell, Bernard 16
O'Donnell, Edward 'Spike' 16–18, 24
O'Donnell, Myles 16, 20, 26
O'Donnell, Steve 16, 18
O'Donnell, Tommy 16, 18, 24
O'Donnell, Walter 16, 18
O'Donnell, William 'Klondike' 16
O'Hare, Edward 48
Oklawaha, Florida 87
Olson, Detective Harold 24

Palace Chop House and Tavern *72*, 73
Palm Beach, Florida 73
Palm Island, Florida *32*, 33, 42, 50
Palmer House Hotel 48
Parker, Bonnie *4*, 89–93, *90–93*
Patton, John 12
Peller, Sam 28
Penn Station, New York City *61*
Pennochio, Tommy 'The Bull' 74–76
Penovich, Peter 22, 50
Petrilli, Dominic 'the Gap' 68
Philadelphia, Pennsylvania 60, 67, 69, 75
Picchi, Frank 46
Pierpont, Harry 80
Pierpont, Indiana police arsenal 80
'Pineapple Primary,' The 33, 36
Pinzolo, Joe 68
Platte City, Missouri 91
Pocahontas, Arkansas 86
Polakoff, Moses 75, 77
Pompez, Alexander 72
Pony Inn 26–27
Pope, Frank 22, 50
Presser, Nancy 77
Probasco, Dr James J 83
Profaci, Joe 67–68
Prohibition 7, 14, 16–17, 29, 48, 56, 59, 62, 64, 67, 72–74
'Public Enemy Number One' 75, 83, 84–85
Purple Gang 36
Purvis, Special Agent Melvin 83–84, 87

Queens, New York 76

Ragen, Frank 17
Ragen's Colts 17
Rathbun, Investigator Charles 44
Ray, James 37
Reed, Public Service Commissioner William 34
Reina, Gaetano 'Tom' 62, 67–68
Reles, Abe 67
Rex Hotel 32
Ricca, 'Paul the Waiter' see Lucia, Felice
Richetti, Adam 84, *87*
Ries, Fred 42, 48, 50
Rio, 'Slippery' Frank 28, 38, 50
Rizzito, Peter 36
'Roaring Twenties' 33
Roa, Joey 72
Roamer Inn 15
Robinson, Edward G 23
Robsky, Paul 40
Roche, State's Attorney Chief Investigator Patrick 43–44, 48
Roosevelt, Governor and President Franklin Delano 70–71
Rosen, Nig 65, 69
Rosencrantz, Bernard 'Lulu' 73
Rosenstiel, Louis 62
Ross, Charles see Luciano, Charlie 'Lucky'
Rothstein, Arnold 59–60, 64–65, 71
Rudensky, 'Red' 53
Rupolo, Ernest 'The Hawk' 74
Russo, Anthony 32

SMC Cartage Company 36–37
Sage, Anna 83
Saietta, Ignazio 7
St Moritz Hotel 67, 70
St Paul, Minnesota 83, 87
St Valentine's Day Massacre 37–38, *37*, 52
Saltis, Joe 'The Pollock' 16, 29–30, 32, 36
Saltis-McErlane Gang 16, 18, 28–29
Sarber, Sheriff Jess 80
'Sawdust Trail' 60
Sawyer, Tom 83
Sbarbo, Assistant State's Attorney John 28
Scalise, Francesco Chiccio see Cheech, Frankie
Scalise, John 16, 21, 24, 25–26, 28–29, 31, 37–38
Scalise, Johnny 62
Scanlon, George 55
Scarface see Capone, Alphonse
Scarpato, Gerardo 68, 70
Schmid, Sheriff Smoot 92
Schoemaker, Detective Chief Dan 30
Schultz, Dutch 58, 64, 72–74, *73*
Schwimmer, Dr Rheinhart H 37
Scotland 59–60
'Scourge of the Underground' see Dewey, Thomas
'Secret Six,' The 40
Seabury, Judge Samuel 71–72
Seager, Sam 40
Security National Bank 82
Serritella, Daniel 31
'Seven Group,' The 65
Shapiro, Jacob 77

Sheldon Gang 28–29,
Sheldon, Ralph 17, 28–30
Shell Oil Building 28
Sheridan Plaza Hotel 48
Sheridan Wave Club 43
Shouse, Edward 80
Shumway, Leslie Albert 'Lou' 48, 50
Sicilian Mafia 6, 55, 60, 68, 70, 78
Sieben Brewery 21–22
Siegel, Benny 'Bugsy' 56, *56*, 60, 64–66, 68, 74–75, 77
Sing Sing Correctional Institution 72, 77
Skidmore, Billy 28, 31
Small, Governor Len 15, 29, 33–34
Small-Thompson-Crowe faction 34
Smith, State Governor Al 36, 66, 71
Smith, Evangelist Gypsy 10
'Snorky' see Alphonse Capone
Solomon, 'King' 65
South Side O'Donnells 15–16, 18
Special Investigations Squad see 'Untouchables, The'
Spicuzza, Vincent 32
Spiller, Bennie 74, 76
Spingola, Henry 25
Stack, Robert 48
'Standard Beverage Corporation, The' 40
Stansbury, Assistant State's Attorney David 38
Staten Island 67
Statue of Liberty *54–55*
Statute of Limitations 48–50
Stege, John 28, 40
Stenson, Joseph 17
Stevens, Walter 15, 18
Sullivan, Special Agent James N 42
Sullivan, Manley 40
Swanson, State's Attorney John A 34, 44
Sweeney, Detective William 24
'Syndicate, The' 70, 78
Syracuse, New York 73

Tammany Hall 7, *8*, 64, 71–72
'Tammany Tiger' see Tammany Hall
Tancl, Eddie 19, 20
Terminal Island Federal Correctional Institution 52
Terranova, Cirro 8, 60, 77
Tessem, Special Agent Nels 42, 46–48
Thompson, William Hale 'Big Bill' 12, 14, 18, 29, 30–31, *31*, 33–36, 44
Thompson submachine gun *4*, 19, 24, *25*, 28, 36, 80, *82*, 84, 87, 88
Thweat, Reverend Silas 52
Time Magazine 83
Times Square, Manhattan 68
'Tommy gun' see Thompson submachine gun
Torchio, Tony 32
Torrio, Johnny 6–15, *17*, 18–22, 24–25, 28, 38, 48, 50, 52, 56, 64- -65, 75
Torrio/Capone Gang 17, 20–21
Tribune, The Chicago 43
Tropea, Orazio 'The Scourge' 16, 24–25
Trotsky, Leon 40
Tuscon, Arizona Police Department 82

Uale, Frank see Yale, Frankie
Unione Siciliane 7, 21–22, 24, 31, 35
Unione Siciliane (Luciano's version) 70
Union Memorial Hospital 52
Union Station, Chicago 48
Union Station, Kansas City 84
US Internal Revenue Service 40
US Department of Justice 40
US Naval Academy 48
US Prohibition Department 40
'Untouchables, The' 40, 44, 48
Untouchables, The (motion picture) *46*
Untouchables, The (television series) *48*
Urchsel, Charles 88

Vacarelli, Paolo Antonino see Kelly, Paul
Vacco, Carmen 21
Valente, Samuel 32
Valentine, Police Commissioner Lewis J 73
Varain, Leland see Alterie, Louie
Vice Commission 10
Victorian Movie Theater 55
Vogel, Eddie 19
Volstead Act 48, 56

Wahrman, Abe 74–76
Wajiechowski, Earl see Weiss, Earl 'Hymie'
Waldorf Towers (Waldorf-Astoria) 70, *70*, 75, 77
Walker, Mayor Jimmy 72
Wall Street Crash of 1929 71
Walsh, Detective Charles 24
'War of Sicilian Succession' 31, 35–36
Warren, Police Commissioner Joseph A 64
Waters, IRS Agent Eddy 40
Weinberg, Bo 73
Weiner, Al 76
Weinshank, Al 36–37
Weiss, Earl 'Hymie' 16, 19, 21, 22, 24, 28
Weiss Gang 22, 24, 28
Western Union 50
West Side O'Donnells 15–16, 19, 24, 26, 28
Wexler, Irving see 'Gordon, Waxey'
Whalen, Police Commissioner Grover 36, 64
Wilkerson, Judge James H 48, 50
Wilson, Tax Investigations Agent Frank 40, 42–43, 46–48
Winchell, Walter 67, 70
Winkler, Gus 38
Winters, Dale 14
White, William 'Three-Fingered Jack' 22
World Series (1919) see 'Black Sox' scandal
Workman, Charlie 'The Bug' 73
Wyoming militia *14*

Yale, Frankie 7, 14, 21, 35–36

Ziegler, George 38
Zion, Eddy 25
Zuta, Jack 31, 43–44
Zwillman, Abner 'Longie' 58, 64, 73